Campground Cookery

Great Recipes For Any Outdoor Activity

Brenda Kulibert

Explorer's Guide Publishing
Rhinelander, Wisconsin

Campground Cookery

Fourth Edition, Revised 1988, 1989, 1991, 1995, 2002
Printed in the United States of America

Published by

Explorer's Guide Publishing
4843 Apperson Drive
Rhinelander, WI 54501
Telephone: (715) 362-6029
Internet: www.explorers-guide.com

ISBN 1-879432-16-1
LCCN 95-060532

I dedicate this book to the memory of my father, Charles R. Phelps, who always had an immense appreciation and respect for the earth's natural resources, and who instilled this love of nature and wildlife in each of his five children.

I would also like to acknowledge and thank the following companies and individuals, without whose help this book would not have been possible

4-H
American Institute for
    Cancer Research
America's Pork Producers
Beef Industry Council
Boy Scouts of America
The Coleman Company
Girl Scouts of America
The Kingsford Company
National Broiler Council
National Fisheries Institute
Pork Industry Group
Reynolds Metals Company
Reynolds Sugar Bush
Rome Industries, Inc.
Sea Grant College Program
UW-Extension

Weber-Stephen Products Co.
Wisconsin Apple Growers
    Association
Wisconsin DATCP Marketing
    Division
Wisconsin DNR
Wisconsin Honey Producers
Wisconsin Milk Marketing
    Board
Wisconsin Regional Cherry
    Growers Association
Wisconsin Turkey Federation

. . . and a *special* thank you to all the wonderful outdoor cooks who shared their favorite recipes with the *Campground Cookery* staff

Contents

Recipes

Getting Started

Breads & Breakfasts

Light Fare

The Main Course

On the Side

Just For Fun

Topping It Off

Appendices

Preface

"There is pleasure in the pathless woods,
There is a rapture on the lonely shore,
There is society, where none intrudes,
By the deep Sea, and music in its roar:
I love not Man the less, but Nature more."

--Lord Byron--

A while back, I was asked by many fellow campers to put my outdoor cooking recipes down in a book. Most knew how to grill a hot dog or hamburger and make simple treats like S'Mores, but they surprisingly knew next to nothing about cooking over a campfire. Fewer still knew anything about Dutch ovens for outdoor cooking. It was then I decided that a cookbook, which taught the basics of outdoor cooking, was needed. That was several years ago, and the beginning of *Campground Cookery*.

What I didn't realize at the time was this book had become *much* more than a little cookbook to bring on camping trips. I found out it was also used for backyard barbecues, family picnics, tailgating parties, and backpacking—any time people got together for a meal outdoors.

Since then, *Campground Cookery* has gone through a few revisions. Some recipes have come and gone, others have been added or edited, and more outdoor cooks from around the country have chosen to donate their favorite recipes to this collection.

In this edition, I have tried to explain the various cooking methods in much greater detail. The introduction has indeed become "A Crash Course in Outdoor Cooking." Hopefully, it will pique the curiosity of many timid outdoor chefs who have, up to this time, only experimented with grilling techniques. A whole new world of cooking with pie irons, foil wraps, and reflector ovens awaits those who are looking for a little variety in their outdoor menus.

As the outdoor cooking industry has continued to grow, so has *Campground Cookery*. While there is yet a real need for many individuals to learn the basics of outdoor cooking, there are also a growing number of outdoor chefs who are looking for more sophisticated recipes. Years ago, campers may have stocked up on hamburgers, hot dogs, and potato chips. Now they are adding exotic mushrooms, tropical fruits, and oriental delicacies to their grocery list. Never before have we had the variety of international foods available to us that we have today, and it is changing the way we look at, and cook, our food.

I hope you enjoy this edition of *Campground Cookery*, and it serves you well in planning your alfresco meals.

Brenda Kulibert

If you want to share recipes, comments or ideas
with the author, she may be reached at
Explorer's Guide Publishing
4843 Apperson Drive
Rhinelander, WI 54501
(715) 362-6029
email: brenda@explorers-guide.com

Introduction

A Crash Course
in Outdoor Cooking

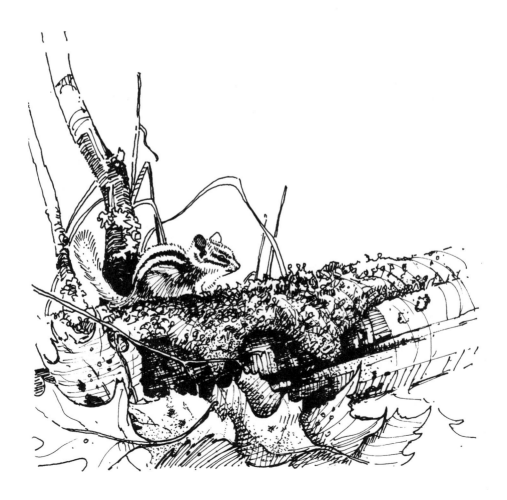

Cooking Over an Open Fire

There are few things more enjoyable then the sight, smells, and sounds of a crackling campfire at the end of the day. It is the gathering place of any camp, especially when it is used for cooking meals. However, if you have problems lighting the fire, some of the enjoyment might "go up in flames." Advance preparation of the site, and proper lighting of the campfire, is essential.

The campfire should be made in a pit surrounded by rocks. After the flames have died down, place a grate over the hot coals, supporting it firmly on the rocks. Food may cook directly on the grate or wrapped in foil. Cooking with foil-wrapped food is described in more detail on page 13.

Dutch oven cooking may also be employed. This versatile pot may rest on top of the grate, be suspended from a tripod, or buried in the hot coals. For more information on Dutch oven cooking, turn to page 21.

With campfire cooking, proper site selection is of the utmost importance. Here are some points to take into consideration.

Campfire Preparation

• Inquire if campfires are permitted in the area. You may need a permit. Check with the local officials, fire department, or the Department of Natural Resources.

• Choose the right spot. Start the fire down wind so the smoke will not blow into the sleeping or eating area. If possible, clear an area of approximately 10 feet around the fire ring. This may seem abnormally large, but sparks emitting from the campfire may ignite dead grass, leaves, and other debris nearby.

• Choose the right fuel. There are three types of wood you will need for your campfire:
> **Tinder:** Twigs and branches smaller than you little finger (dried grass or pine needles).
> **Kindling:** Wood the size of your little finger to the size of your wrist.
> **Fuel:** Pieces of wood the size of your wrist and larger.
Split, dry wood provides the most efficient heat and is the easiest for lighting. Dried hardwoods such as oak, maple, and hickory are your best choices. The use of pine for campfire cooking will add the unpleasant taste of pitch to unwrapped foods cooked over the fire.

• Use a good supply of tinder and kindling. Paper, dry wood shavings (not sawdust), and thinly stripped pieces of wood make the best kindling. They will light easily and burn quickly, igniting the larger pieces of wood.

• You will need **dry or waterproof matches** to light the fire. Pack your matches in a waterproof zip lock plastic bag before your camping trip.

Once you have selected just the right site, you can start the fire. Here's the correct way of going about it.

Starting the Campfire

1. Arrange a small stack of kindling into a pyramid shape. Light in several places to start the fire quickly. *Do not use gas or kerosene.* Both pose a serious danger of explosion.

2. Add larger sticks as the fire builds. Quickly adding too much wood will restrict the air flow to the fire.

3. Put the largest pieces of wood or split logs on last, resting carefully on top of the already burning pieces of wood. Exercise caution. Throwing wood on the fire may result in a sudden shower of sparks.

4. To keep the fire burning, arrange larger pieces of wood around the outside of the fire. Gradually push them into the flames.

5. When the fire has burned to a bed of hot coals you are ready to start cooking. A smoldering fire, or one with a lot of flames, will not provide the most efficient heat. This type of fire will also cover your pots and pans with soot. (The exception to this rule is in reflector oven cooking. The oven's shiny surface reflects the heat from the campfire back into the oven to bake the food. While you do not need a "roaring" fire, flames are needed to cook the food properly. For more information, turn to page 23.)

6. **Never leave your fire unattended. Keep a bucket of dirt or water and a shovel nearby in case of an emergency.**

7. Meals may be prepared over an open fire using a variety of methods: on a grate supported by rocks, in a Dutch oven placed in the coals, foil wrapped and placed in the coals, in a reflector oven placed near the campfire, or in a pot suspended below a tripod.

8. Put the fire out when you are finished cooking. Use plenty of water, not just a sprinkling. All the coals, embers, and wood must be wet and cooled. If a fire starts due to carelessness, you will be responsible for any damages.

"Remember, only you can prevent forest fires."
(Smoky Bear takes this very seriously!)

Grilling

Charcoal Grills

Charcoal grilling is undoubtedly the most popular outdoor cooking method. It used to mean slapping a couple hot dogs and hamburgers on the grill at the family picnic. Today, grilling is an art form in itself.

Any type of food can be prepared on a charcoal grill, with unsurpassed results. Hot dogs have given way to exotic seafoods. Good, old-fashioned grilled corn on the cob has given way to marinated zucchini strips and portabella mushrooms. Meals can be grilled, smoked, steamed, stir-fried, baked, or boiled to perfection. This is definitely NOT your dad's old Sunday barbecue anymore!

Charcoal grills are available in a wide variety of models—from small hibachis to large, covered kettle-type grills. This diversity of grills, gourmet foods, and new breed of outdoor chefs has spawned a multi-billion dollar gourmet grilling industry worldwide. The "barbie" is as much a part of Australian life as the 4th of July picnic is in America.

Starting the Charcoal Grill

Before you begin, check to see if you have enough charcoal briquets to completely cook the meal. Usually, 30 briquets will cook a pound of meat on a kettle grill. You will need approximately:

> **60 briquets for a large grill (26")***
> **32 briquets for a medium grill (18")***
> **20 briquets for a small grill (14")***

*Open grills and hibachis may require additional briquets.

If your recipe calls for a long cooking time (more than an hour) you will need to add more briquets during cooking. Using long-handled tongs, place 10-12 briquets at the outer edge of the hot coals after cooking for about 30 minutes. When a fine, white ash covers these coals, add them to the center of the fire to maintain a constant temperature.

1. First, stack briquets into a pyramid.

2. Pretreat briquets with at least one-half cup of starter fluid. Let it soak into the charcoal for about a minute before lighting. Use only liquid charcoal starters. (Pretreated charcoal briquets, such as Matchlight® charcoal briquets from Kingsford®, are very handy and do not require additional lighter fluid to start.) *Do not use gasoline or kerosene to start the coals. Both are dangerous and may flare up.*

3. If you need to relight the briquets, **do not add starter fuel to hot charcoal.** Instead take two or three additional briquets, place them in a container, and add some lighter fluid. When they have absorbed the fuel (1 to 2 minutes), place them on the pyramid in the grill and light. Do not add the remaining fuel to the hot briquets.

4. The coals are ready when they are covered with white ash. This takes about 25 to 30 minutes.

Note: Cooking with charcoal uses oxygen and releases toxic fumes into the air. **NEVER** *cook indoors, not even in an open garage. Inhaling toxic fumes may be fatal.*

Gauging the Temperature of Hot Coals

Just as it is important to know the temperature of your oven or stove, it is important to know the approximate temperature of coals when grilling with charcoal. Improperly gauging the temperature of the coals may result in tough, overcooked meats.

First, let the flames die down. A fine white ash will cover the coals in 20-30 minutes.

Then, carefully place your hand about 6 inches above the coals. Start counting the seconds: "one-one thousand, two-one thousand, three-one thousand." Note the time it takes before you need to withdraw your hand.

Using the table below, find the approximate temperature of the coals.

Time elapsed before withdrawing hand	Coals are	Approximate temperature
2 seconds	Hot	400°
3 seconds	Medium-hot	375°
4 seconds	Medium	350°
5 seconds	Medium-low	325°
6 seconds	Low	300°

Gas Grills

With gas grills now within the price range of most outdoor chefs, gas grilling is developing quite a following. It provides all the wonderful taste of charcoal grilling without all the mess—in a word, convenience.

Gas grills are also available in a wide variety of models. Grills will have one to three burners. Any of these work well for grilling. The heat source is a cylinder of propane gas attached to the grill. The temperature is regulated by the simple turn of a knob.

It is important to read the operating instructions of your particular gas grill before using. Routinely clean and properly maintain your grill for best performance.

Direct vs Indirect Grilling

It doesn't matter if you have a gas or charcoal grill, certain types of food should be grilled directly over the heat source, while others should be grilled indirectly. In general—

- **Direct heat** is recommended for thinner cuts of meat, fish, poultry, and vegetables that require hot temperatures and quick cooking times.
- **Indirect heat** is recommended for large cuts of meat that require longer cooking times, such as roasts, hams, turkeys, and whole fish.

Here's how to do both.

Indirect Grilling — Covered Charcoal Grills

1. Open bottom grill vents. This will keep air circulating around the hot coals.
2. Pile an equal number of coals on either side of the bottom grate.

3. Place an aluminum drip pan (with a small amount of water added) on the bottom grate between the two piles of coals. This will catch the grease dripping from the grilling food.
4. Light the coals as directed. When the coals are covered with a fine, white ash replace the cooking grate.
5. Place the meat on the cooking grate over the aluminum pan. Fat from the meat will drip into the pan below. Cover the grill, making sure the top vent is open.
6. Grill as directed.

Indirect Grilling — Gas Grills

One-Burner Grills
1. Place the drip pan under the cooking area. Add a small amount of water to the drip pan to prevent splattering.
2. Grill the meat with low to medium heat, directly over the drip pan.

Two-Burner Grills
1. Turn one side burner off and set the other on low to medium heat.
2. Place an aluminum drip pan under the cooking area (side that is turned off). Add a small amount of water to the drip pan to prevent splattering.
3. Place meat on the cooking area directly above the drip pan.
4. Grill as directed.

Three-Burner Grills
1. Turn the middle burner off and set the other two burners on low to medium heat.
2. Place an aluminum drip pan in the center under the cooking area. Add a small amount of water to the drip pan to prevent splattering.
3. Place meat on the cooking area directly above the drip pan.
4. Grill as directed.

Direct Grilling — Covered Charcoal Grills

1. Open bottom vents. This will keep air circulating around the hot coals.
2. Place coals in a pyramid on the bottom grate and light, following charcoal manufacturer's instructions.
3. When the coals are covered with a fine, white ash, spread evenly over the bottom grate. Replace the cooking grate.
4. Place food on the cooking surface directly above the hot coals. Cover, and grill as directed.

Direct Grilling — Gas Grills

1. Turn burners on medium to high heat.
2. Place food on the cooking surface directly above the burners.
3. Grill as directed.

Some Helpful Grilling Tips

- Always brush the cooking surface (top grate) with salad oil, bacon drippings, or fat trimmed from the meat to be cooked. This will help prevent food from sticking to the grill and make cleanup a snap.

- Parboil solid or starchy vegetables before skewering. When combining meat with fruit or vegetables, use small pieces of meat. Meat and vegetables will cook evenly.

- Before grilling, baste lean meats, fish, and poultry with butter, salad dressing, marinades, or olive oil. Turn often to prevent the meat from drying out and burning.

- Trim excess fat from the outer edge of meats so the dripping fat will not cause the coals to flare up.

- Score the edges of steaks, chops, or ham to prevent the edges from curling up.

- Steaks are ready to turn when juices appear on the uncooked surface. Fat on the edge of the meat will appear translucent and juices will be bubbling.

- Season meats after grilling. Salt draws out juices and will toughen the meat. Use tongs for turning instead of a fork, which punctures the meat and allows juices to escape.

- Grill chicken halves or pieces bone side down, first. The bones help distribute heat throughout the meats.

- Cook foods that are relatively thin, such as steaks, hamburgers, or cut-up chicken, using direct heat. Whole meats such as chickens, hams, or roasts require the use of indirect heat. Heat reflects off the top of the grill, cooking the meat on all sides at once.

- The fire is hot (325° to 400° Fahrenheit), and the heat transfers to the cooking utensils, the grill, and the cooking food. Always wear heavy mitts when cooking or handling any part of the grill, and always exercise caution.

The Art of Foil Cooking

Foil cooking is done by wrapping food in aluminum foil, then cooking over, or in, a bed of hot coals. The foil holds in juices and flavor, and allows direct cooking on hot coals with minimal risk of burning. Aluminum foil also creates easy-to-make pots and pans, reducing the need for additional dishes—a big plus in camping.

Aluminum foil comes in regular and heavy duty thicknesses. Ordinarily, heavy-duty aluminum foil is recommended for foil cooking. If all you have is the regular thickness, simply double it.

You can cook practically any type of food in foil, making camp menus varied and interesting. The key to foil cooking is the use of different folds and wraps to hold in the natural juices.

Wrapping the Food Packages

There are two basic ways of wrapping food in aluminum foil, the drugstore wrap and the bundle wrap. Either way will seal in the juices and prevent dirt and ashes from coming in contact with the food.

Drugstore Wrap

1. Place food in center of a sheet of Heavy Duty Reynolds Wrap® aluminum foil large enough to permit adequate wrapping.

2. Bring two sides of foil up over food. For cooking, fold down loosely in a series of locked folds, allowing for heat circulation and expansion. For freezing, fold down in a series of locked folds, until foil is tight against food.

3. Fold short ends up and over again; crimp to seal.

Bundle Wrap

1. Center food on a square of Heavy Duty Reynolds Wrap® aluminum foil large enough for adequate wrapping.

2. Bring four corners of foil up together in a pyramid shape.

Illustrations from:
Reynolds Metals Company

3. Fold the open edges together in locked folds. For cooking, fold loosely, allowing for heat circulation and expansion. For freezing, fold tightly, pressing air out until foil is tight against food.

Creating Cooking Utensils

Next time you go camping, try making these handy cooking utensils out of aluminum foil. It's easy and fun. Here's how.

Coat Hanger Griddle

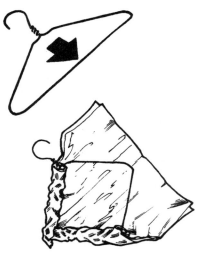

1. Pull bottom of coat hanger into a square of wire. Bend the hook downward to make a handle.

2. Center hanger on two sheets of Heavy Reynolds Wrap® 1^1/$_2$ times the size of square. Roll each side toward wire rims, crimping until secure.

3. Turn griddle over; depress the center slightly to form a well to hold food.

4. To use, prop griddle on rocks over hot embers.

CAUTION: Always use pot holders when handing hot griddle.

Illustrations from: Reynolds Metals Company

Forked Stick Frying Pan

1. Use a forked stick with prongs wide enough to contain food. Center stick on two sheets of Heavy Duty Reynolds Wrap® double the width of the fork opening.

2. Starting at bottom corners, roll foil diagonally toward fork; crimp securely around each side of fork. Roll top edge down.

3. Turn forked stick over; depress the center slightly to form a well to hold food and to keep liquids from running off. Roll a sheet of Heavy Duty Reynolds Wrap® around neck of pan handle to protect stick from fire.

4. To use, frying pan can be propped over hot embers by resting on rocks.

Illustrations from:
Reynolds Metals Company

Saucepan and Mixing/ Serving Bowl

1. Mold three layers of Heavy Duty Reynolds Wrap® aluminum foil around a straight-sided bowl or canister to form desired size. At campsite, mold foil around a one-gallon drinking cooler or end of a log.

2. Remove bowl or cooler. Crimp down edge to form a tight rim.

3. To use, place on barbecue grill. At campsite, place on a metal rack supported by rocks over hot embers. To remove, use pot holders in both hands.

Illustrations from:
Reynolds Metals Company

Reflector Oven

1. Insert two Y-shaped sticks, about 18" apart, firmly into the ground at the edge of the fire ring, and close enough so the heat of the fire is reflected into the oven.

2. Remove Reynolds Wrap® from box. Wrap the end around a straight 22" stick and place across Y-shaped openings.

3. Unroll foil sheet down toward the ground at a 45° angle. Lay another 22" stick at ground level to hold the foil secure. Bring remaining foil forward allowing enough space on the foil behind the Y-shaped sticks to hold a baking rack. Tear off sheet.

Illustrations from:
Reynolds Metals Company

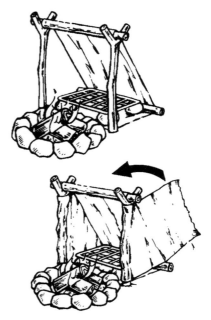

4. Rest the baking rack on four rocks in the oven.

5. For the side panel, wrap the 18" edge of foil to the Y stick. Extend to the center back of oven. Tear off sheet. Repeat with other Y stick.

6. Fold sheets together starting at the upper corner and folding toward back of oven.

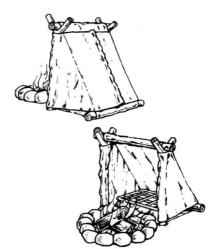

7. To use, open the oven by unfolding one side panel at the back of the oven. Secure again quickly to prevent heat loss.

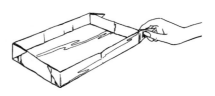

Drip Pan or Baking Sheet

1. Use two sheets of Heavy Duty Reynolds Wrap® aluminum foil 6 inches longer and 6 inches wider than the desired size of pan. Fold in all edges $1\frac{1}{2}$ to 2 inches.

2. Score corners.

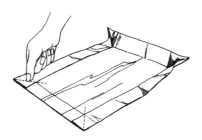

3. Fold again forming $1\frac{1}{2}$ to 2 inch sides and miter corners against side of pans. For drip pan, carefully place between hot coals in fire bowl. Let fat cool before removing pan from grill. For baking sheet, place on grill rack over coals.

Illustrations from:
Reynolds Metals Company

Cooking in Foil

Once you are ready to cook a foil wrapped meal, you need a bed of hot coals. Hardwoods such as oak, maple, and elm produce the best heat if you are cooking over an open fire. The fire is ready after the flames have died down and only hot, glowing coals remain.

When using a grill, make sure the coals are hot and covered with a white ash before cooking the food. If the cooking time is longer than an hour you may need to add more coals each hour.

To cook your foil wrapped meal in hot coals, dig a hole in the hot coals that is large enough to contain the package. Rake the coals over. For even cooking on all sides, place each package in a separate hole.

Remove the packages from the coals using long-handled tongs or a forked stick when you are finished cooking. Remember, these packages are very HOT! Let the food cool for several minutes, then carefully open the package, letting the steam escape. Serve food right from the foil or on plates. Oven mitts are advisable when handling these meals.

Cooking Tips for Foil Wrapped Meals

- Add a teaspoon of salad oil, shortening, butter, or bacon to meats to prevent sticking and burning. Add a tablespoon of water to vegetables for the same purpose.
- Meats and vegetables may cook together to save time and foil. Slice, dice, or shoestring vegetables when cooking them with meats, since they require a longer cooking time.
- Hamburgers, steaks, and chops cook in 15 to 20 minutes, but pork and lamb chops take a little longer.
- Roasts and large game birds require more than an hour to cook.
- Small to medium fish fillets are cooked completely in about 15 minutes, depending on the size.

Dutch Oven Cooking

Dutch ovens are one of the more versatile appliances for cooking outdoors. You can roast, bake, stew, boil, slow cook, or fry in a Dutch oven. These pots can be buried in the coals, cooked on top of the coals, or suspended from a tripod above the coals. The lid also serves as an impromptu fry pan when flipped upside down and nestled on hot coals.

Dutch ovens have been used in America since colonial times. A large, cast iron pot was fashioned so it could be placed directly on hot coals. By placing additional hot coals on top of the flat lid, the Dutch oven could be used for roasting and baking.

There are several designs of Dutch ovens on the market today. All are constructed of heavy cast iron for even heat distribution. However, the best design for cooking in an open fire features a flat, slightly flanged lid, flat bottom, and three to four short legs jutting out from the bottom of the pot about two inches.

Dutch ovens vary in size, so purchase the one that is the right size for you. Because cast iron is quite heavy, you don't want to be carrying around an oven that is larger than you actually need.

Before using your Dutch oven for the first time, it must be washed thoroughly, and then "seasoned." Follow the manufacturer's directions for proper seasoning, or use the method below.

Thoroughly coat the inside of the pot and lid with vegetable oil. Place in a preheated moderate (350°) oven and bake for one hour, brushing the inside surfaces with additional oil every 15 minutes or so. Once the pot is properly seasoned, it will only need to be lightly washed, not scrubbed. The smoked oil seals the porous surface so foods will not stick. If, over time, food does begin to stick, simply wash and repeat the seasoning process. Your Dutch oven should last a lifetime.

As a Slow Cooker

1. Start a good campfire. Coals should be glowing hot.
2. Prepare your stew or whatever meal you would like to slow cook.
3. Clear an area five feet in diameter of leaves, sticks, and other debris. Dig a pit about 1$^1/_2$ feet in diameter, and 2 feet deep.
4. Shovel about 6-8 inches of red-hot, glowing coals into the bottom of the pit. Lower the covered Dutch oven on top of the coals, making sure the wire bail to the pot (not the lid) is sitting upright.
5. Surround and cover the Dutch oven with additional hot coals. Top the coals loosely with an inch or so of dirt. Do not pack tightly in or the dirt will smother the coals.
6. Your stew will slow cook all day, and should not burn.
7. To excavate your meal, brush dirt off of lid. Lift the Dutch oven carefully out of the pit by its wire bail, not the lid handle (or your meal will be covered with dirt and ruined.)
8. The pot will be extremely hot, so use caution, and heavy oven mitts.

For Baking

1. Start a good campfire. The coals should be glowing hot.
2. Prepare your favorite recipe for baked goods, or place ready-made, unbaked goods in the bottom of the Dutch oven. You may wish to first place them in a small round cake pan or on a rack nestled in the bottom of the pot.
3. Cover the pot and bury in a pit surrounded by hot coals or simply bury in the middle of the hot coals in the campfire.
4. Follow individual recipes for cooking times.

Reflector Oven Cooking

Reflector ovens are constructed from polished aluminum or sheet metal. (For instructions on how to make your own reflector oven out of aluminum foil, turn to page 18.) Heat from the campfire is reflected into the nearby oven and around the food.

How It Works

Wait until the flames die down a bit, then place the reflector oven near the campfire (about 12 inches away, to start). Then, to achieve the best results, wrap a sheet of heavy duty aluminum foil, shiny side up, over a baking sheet. Prop upright across the fire from the reflector oven. A steady stream of heat will reflect back into the oven, toasting food to a golden brown.

Gauging the Temperature Inside the Oven

To adjust the temperature of the oven, simply move the oven closer to, or further away from the fire as necessary. An easy way to roughly gauge the temperature inside the oven is as follows. Place your hand directly in front of the oven. Start counting the seconds: "one-one thousand, two-one thousand, three-one thousand." Note the time it takes before you need to withdraw your hand.

Using the table on the next page, find the approximate temperature inside the oven.

Time elapsed before withdrawing hand	Oven is	Approximate temperature
1-2 seconds	Hot	500°
3-4 seconds	Medium-hot	400°
5-6 seconds	Medium	300°
7-10 seconds	Low	200°

Care of Your Reflector Oven

Because heat is reflected from the shiny surfaces of the oven and onto the food, it is important that the walls of the oven be kept clean for the oven to work efficiently. After each use, wipe off any food that has spilled onto the oven. Then, wash the oven with a soft cloth and nonabrasive soap to remove any further residue. Rinse and dry thoroughly, wrap in a towel, and store in a soft cloth bag.

(After time, smoke from the campfire will tend to dull the surface. If this happens, rub lightly with a nonabrasive cleanser to bring back the shine.)

Special Hints

• To prevent messy cleanups, place food in aluminum pans before setting in the oven

• For even browning, rotate food every few minutes

• Thaw frozen foods before baking in the oven

• Arrange individual items, such as muffins, cookies, rolls, etc., evenly inside the oven. Leave enough space around each item for the hot air to circulate.

• Prepackaged cookie dough bakes up very nicely in reflector ovens. Simply cut and arrange on a baking sheet. Bake until golden brown.

• Just as in any oven, baked food will be very hot. Use oven mitts or tongs to remove food.

• If you are cooking for a larger group or would like to bake two things at once, two reflector ovens may be used. Place the second oven directly across the fire from the first. Heat will reflect off back and forth from one oven to the other, eliminating the need for the foil-lined baking sheet as a backdrop.

Other Handy Appliances

Camp Stoves

Camp stoves are portable stoves which are fueled by gas or propane. They can be taken anywhere you go, are easy to operate, and provide a quick cooking source when you are tired and hungry from a day on the trail.

Temperature is adjusted by a valve on the side or front of the stove. A cylinder of fuel will burn for one to eight hours, depending on the model of the stove and cooking temperature.

Stoves range in size from the ultralight, one-burner backpacking models to the larger, rectangular, multi-burner models. Some models provide easy, matchless lighting in high-moisture environments and in temperatures down to freezing.

Pie Irons

Pie irons, also called sandwich cookers or pudgie pie makers, are heavy, cast aluminum two-piece pans with long handles. They are designed to seal fillings between two slices of bread, creating a warm, delicious, hand-held meal. (Before using for the first time, wash completely and brush the inside with cooking oil.)

To use, place a slice of bread, buttered side down, in the pie iron. Top with desired filling and another slice of bread, buttered side up. Close the iron, latch handle; trim off excess bread if necessary. Cook over medium coals until golden brown on both sides (about 3 to 6 minutes). After each use, simply wipe with a paper towel and wash off any filling that may have spilled out.

Getting Started

Beverages
Snacks and Trail Mixes
Snacks for Backpacking

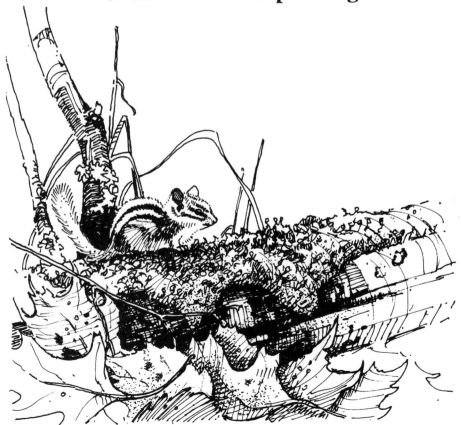

BEVERAGES

Chocolate
Hot Chocolate, Variations

Next time you make hot chocolate, try one of the following variations.

To a cup of hot chocolate add one of these:
- **Crushed peppermint candies**
- **Dash of Amaretto liqueur**
- **Dash of rum**
- **1 Tbsp pure maple syrup**
- **Cinnamon stick**

Coffee
Camp Coffee

Ground coffee
Egg shells
Water

Use 2 heaping teaspoons of coffee for each cup of water. Put the coffee in the pot with a few egg shells and a little cold water. Stir gently, then add remaining water. Place the coffee pot on a grate over the campfire. When the coffee boils up, move the pot off to the side of the grate, away from direct flames. Allow the coffee to settle over low heat for 10 minutes. Strain and serve.

Fruit Drinks
Cran-Apple Toastie

2 cups cranberry juice cocktail
2 cups apple cider
4 cinnamon sticks

Place a cinnamon stick in each cup. Slowly warm juices in a pan over low heat. When warmed through, pour into the cups containing the cinnamon sticks. Makes four 1-cup servings.

Hot Apple Cider

6 cups cider
1 to 2 sticks cinnamon
$^1/_2$ tsp whole cloves

Heat all ingredients in a saucepan, simmering for 5 minutes. Makes 6 servings.

Variation: Add a twist of lemon, or eliminate spices and add $^1/_8$ cup red cinnamon candies.

Hot Apple-Orange Drink

Apple juice
Orange juice
Cinnamon sticks or red hot candies

Mix equal parts of apple juice and orange juice. Warm in a saucepan over low heat. Place a cinnamon stick, or a few red hot candies, into a cup and pour juices over. Serve warm.

Hot Lemonade

Instant lemonade mix
Hot water

Instead of making your favorite lemonade with cold water, make it with hot water. It makes a delicious warm drink on cold mornings, and is especially soothing for scratchy throats.

Variation: Substitute orange drink mix for lemonade. Add a little to your cup, cover with boiling water, and stir.

Orange Julius

1 Tbsp malted milk powder
Juice of two oranges
1 tsp sugar or honey
Water
Nutmeg

Mix malted milk powder, orange juice, and sugar (or honey) in a plastic shaker bottle. Add 6-8 ounces icy cold water. Shake well to blend. Top with a dash of nutmeg.

Refreshing Watermelon Cocktail

Watermelon pieces, cut into bite-sized chunks
Sugar
Lemon juice
Ginger ale

Place watermelon pieces in a bowl with a little sugar and lemon juice; stir. Arrange in an 8-oz cup. Pour ginger ale over fruit to serve.

Quick Apple Drink

4 scoops pre-sweetened apple Kool Aid®
2 cups water
2 cups prepared orange juice
7 Up®

Mix the first three ingredients in a 2-quart plastic or glass pitcher. Chill. Just before serving, add 7 Up® to desired taste.

Teas

Friendship Tea

2 cups orange flavored drink mix
$^1/_2$ cup instant tea
1 packet instant lemonade mix
$1^1/_2$ cups sugar
1 tsp cinnamon
$^1/_4$ tsp ground cloves

Combine all ingredients in an airtight container. Will keep for several weeks. Before using, stir contents thoroughly. Place 2 teaspoons of mix into a cup of boiling water. Stir until powders thoroughly dissolve.

Iced Sun Tea

Place several tea bags in a glass or clear plastic water bottle. Fill the bottle with water and place it in full sun for 2-3 hours. Next, secure the bottle in a cool stream, or wrap with a damp towel and place in the shade. To serve, fill a glass with crushed ice. Pour the sun tea over the ice. Serve immediately.

SNACKS and TRAIL MIXES

Snacks
Apple-Peanut Butter Slices

4 med-size, firm apples
4-6 Tbsp peanut butter (creamy or crunchy)

Wash and core apples. Spoon $1\frac{1}{2}$ tablespoons peanut butter into the center cavity of each apple. Wrap apples in plastic wrap and chill for 4-6 hours. Remove plastic wrap and slice each apple crosswise into $\frac{1}{2}$-inch slices. Rewrap apples and chill again until ready to serve. Makes 4 servings.

Variation: Use processed cheese spread instead of peanut butter.

Campfire Popcorn

$\frac{1}{4}$ cup popcorn
2 Tbsp salad oil
$\frac{1}{4}$ tsp salt

Place popcorn, salad oil, and salt in the center of an 18-inch square piece of heavy-duty aluminum foil. Form into a bundle, leaving enough room for the popcorn to pop when cooking.

Wire the bundle to a long sturdy stick. Cook over the camp-fire, or place directly on coals by grasping the top of the bundle with tongs. Shake continuously until the corn stops popping, then remove from heat.

Carefully peel back the hot foil. Enjoy the popcorn directly out of the foil bundle. Add salt and/or butter if desired.

Mexican Munchies

Make at home and carry to the campsite in air tight bags.

$1/2$ cup butter or margarine
2 cans french fried onion rings
14-oz shoestring potato sticks
1 pkg taco seasoning
2 lbs mixed nuts or peanuts

Preheat oven to 275°. Melt butter in a roasting pan. Add remaining ingredients, stirring well.

Bake for 45 minutes, stirring every 10 minutes, then remove from oven. When cool, place in an airtight container.

Muesli Bars

$1/2$ cup brown sugar
5 Tbsp water
1 cup oatmeal
$1/2$ cup toasted chopped almonds
$1/4$ cup toasted chopped pecans
$1/8$ cup All Bran® cereal
$1/8$ cup sesame seeds
3 Tbsp honey

Grease a 9x9-inch pan; set aside. Combine sugar and water in a large saucepan. Stir over medium heat until sugar dissolves. Bring to a boil. Cook for 3 minutes, stirring constantly, then remove from heat. Add remaining ingredients, blending well. Spoon into the prepared pan; pat down. Cool, and cut into bars. Makes 20 bars.

Nachos

1 bag tortilla chips
Sharp cheddar cheese, shredded
Chili or jalepenos peppers, finely chopped
Black olives, chopped
1 medium onion, finely chopped
1 ripe tomato, chopped and drained

Shape a tray out of heavy duty aluminum foil or purchase a pre-made aluminum tray. Arrange tortilla chips on the bottom. Sprinkle with cheese. Top with peppers, olives, onion, and tomato. Bake on a grate in a reflector oven until cheese is melted and bubbly.

Toasted Pumpkin Seeds

4 cups pumpkin seeds
2 Tbsp butter
2 Tbsp peanut oil
4 Tbsp salt

Preheat oven to 250° F. Wash pumpkin seeds and pat dry. Combine all ingredients and spread in an ungreased roasting pan.

Roast for 45 minutes, or until seeds are a golden brown, stirring every 15 minutes. Remove from oven and cool. Store in air tight bags. Great alone or can be combined with salted sunflower seeds for a quick snack on the trail.

Trail Mixes, Gorp
Cereal Survival Necklace

Kids love helping with this recipe. They not only have fun making something yummy for the trail, but they even get to wear their food!

Dry breakfast cereal that has a hole in it,
   such as Cheerios®, Honeycomb®, Fruit Loops®
Assorted dried fruit
String or yarn - 18 inches long
Needle

Thread the cereal and fruit onto the string. Knot the string securely. Wear as a necklace when you are hiking. When you need a little "energy boost," take a nibble from the necklace. The snacks are right at hand.

Gorp

Hikers and backpackers have always been a hearty, enterprising lot. The need for a quick, easy, and energy-boosting snack on the trail led to a phenomenon called Gorp, an abbreviation of "good old raisins and peanuts." While it is a pretty basic recipe of dried fruits, nuts, and grains, home-made gorp reflects the preferences of the maker. In other words, "If you like it, throw it in."

1 cup quick-cooking rolled oats
1 cup shelled peanuts
$^1/_2$ cup shredded coconut
$^1/_4$ cup wheat germ
$^1/_2$ cup honey
2 Tbsp cooking oil
1 cup chocolate chips
$^1/_2$ cup coarsely chopped dried fruit
$^1/_2$ cup raisins

Combine oats, nuts, coconut, and wheat germ in a medium bowl. In a small bowl combine honey and oil. Stir into oat mixture, blending well. Spread on a greased baking sheet.

Bake at 300° for 30-40 minutes, stirring every 15 minutes. Remove from oven, cool, and break into large chunks. Combine with chocolate, fruit and raisins. Store in tightly covered containers.

Hawaiian-Style Gorp

1 jar macadamia nuts, halved
1 cup shredded coconut, toasted
1 cup dried pineapple
1 cup dried bananas
1 cup honey roasted peanuts

Combine all ingredients. Store in airtight bags.

Heidi's Trail Mix

1 cup dry cereal of choice
1 cup peanuts or soy nuts
1 handful pretzel sticks
1 cup raisins
Handful of dried fruit

Combine all ingredients. Store in airtight bags.

M & M's® Trail Mix

1½ cup dried apples
1½ cup M & M's® (or carob pieces)
1 cup peanuts (or nut of choice)
1 cup raisins or dates, chopped

Combine all ingredients. Store in airtight bags.

Trail Bars

1 cup sesame seeds
½ cup chopped nuts (unsalted)
½ cup sunflower or pumpkin seeds
½ cup firmly packed brown sugar
½ cup honey
½ cup dates or raisins
½ cup dried apples or apricots
½ cup unsweetened shredded coconut
Butter

Combine sesame seeds, chopped nuts, and sunflower seeds. Spread in a thin layer on a rimmed baking sheet. Roast in a 300° F oven for 15 minutes (or until lightly browned), shaking baking sheet occasionally. Remove from oven and set aside.

Combine brown sugar, honey, and dried fruits in a wide frying pan. Bring mixture to a boil over medium heat, stirring constantly. Cook 2 minutes, then remove from heat. Stir in seeds, nuts, and coconut, mixing thoroughly.

Turn out onto a shallow 9x11-inch pan. Press mixture firmly and evenly over the bottom of the pan with a large buttered spoon or sheet of waxed paper.

Cool at room temperature for 30 minutes. Lift out with a wide spatula and cut into bars. Store at room temperature.

BACKPACKING SNACKS

Hiking, backpacking, and prolonged exposure to the elements all increase the body's demand for additional energy. The standard three meals a day may not produce enough fuel to keep up with your body's metabolic demands. Small, frequent meals are better for your digestion than three large meals per day. Therefore, a well-chosen nutritional snack on the trail will give you an energy boost when you need it most.

Increased fluid intake is also very important in your backpacking diet, especially if you are eating dehydrated or salty foods, or if the weather is hot and dry. Avoid alcoholic beverages, as well as beverages containing a lot of caffeine or sugar. They will sap your energy, and will not quench your thirst as well as water, juices, or sports drinks.

Trail mixes and gorp are especially suited for long hikes, and are perfect for tucking in your pack. Listed below are some additional ideas for quick snacks that are as nutritious as they are delicious.

- **fruit leathers** (recipe on p. 39)
- **raisins, dried cranberries*, and dried cherries***
- **dried fruits**
- **fresh fruits**
- **fresh bite-sized vegetables**
- **roasted nuts**
- **toasted pumpkin seeds** (recipe on p. 34)
- **toasted sunflower seeds**

* Dried cranberries and recipes are available from the Cranberry Gift House, 339 W Pine St., Eagle River, WI 54521, (800) 285-8806; or from Ocean Spray Cranberries, Inc., Ocean Spray Consumer Affairs Dept., One Ocean Spray Dr., Lakeville-Middleboro, MA 02349, (800) 662-3263, www.oceanspray.com.

*Dried cherries and recipes are available from Country Ovens, Ltd., P.O. Box 195, Forestville, WI 54213, (920) 856-6767, www.countryovens.com; or from Sunrise Dried Fruit Co., (800) 488-5762, www.sunrisedriedfruit.com.

Carbohydrates on the Trail

The food we eat can be broken down into three main categories—proteins, fats and carbohydrates. All three are essential for a healthy diet. However, only carbohydrates digest rapidly and easily, providing needed "instant energy" on the trail. This is the reason most trail mixes are composed mainly of carbohydrates such as fruits, cereals, sugars, starches, and candy. Eat small amounts of trail mix frequently for an energy boost.

Fruit Leathers

Fruit leathers (fruit roll-ups) are pliable, portable, sheets of dried, pureéd fruit which provide the goodness of fruit without all the bulk. When you are carrying a pack on the trail, weight becomes a very important consideration.

Leathers may be made with vitually any type of fruit, but those in which the seeds can be readily removed seems to work the best.

Sun-Dried Fruit Leathers

If you are on an extended camping trip and have access to a local farmer's market, you may want to try your hand at drying the fruit naturally outdoors. You will need lots of direct sunlight, so don't start this project on rainy or cloudy days.

Begin by purchasing fully ripe, unbruised fruit. Since you won't have access to a food processor at camp, softer fruit such as bananas, peaches, plums, and pears (or a combination), will work the best. (However, canned applesauce or jars of pureéd fruit for babies also works very well, without all the extra fuss.)

Clean, peel, and core the fruit, then chop into manageable pieces. If necessary, sweeten to taste with a little sugar or honey (also helps bind fruit together.) Place fruit in a pot and quickly bring to a boil just to dissolve the sugar. Remove from heat. When cool enough to handle, mash fruit to a pulp using a potato masher.

Line a baking sheet with plastic wrap. If you don't have a baking sheet, place sheets of heavy duty aluminum foil on a level surface (picnic table). Cover foil with plastic wrap. Spoon the fruit pulp onto the plastic wrap. Using the back of the spoon, spread the pulp evenly to within 2 inches of the edge. **Note: Fruit layer should be no more than $1/4$-inch thick.**

Cover with a layer of cheesecloth held a few inches away from the fruit to protect it from bugs and leaves. Place in full sunlight, bringing in at night (if possible). Drying time depends on the water content of the fruit and the thickness of the layer. However, most fruit leathers will sun-dry in about 24 hours. Fruit will be pliable and leathery, and not sticky to the touch when done. To store, leave the leather on the plastic wrap and roll up, tucking in sides as you go.

Using a Dehydrator

If you want to prepare fruit leathers at home, commercially available dehydrators do a very nice job. **Note: While sweeteners do help bind the fruit together, they will also increase the chances of burning the leather, so use with caution.**

Prepare the fruit as directed in the sun-drying instructions. You may want to pureé the fruit in a food processor instead of using a potato masher.

Line dehydrator trays with plastic wrap, allowing extra wrap at the ends and sides, and taking care not to cover the center hole of dehydrator. Pour a small amount of fruit pureé into the center of the wrap and spread thinly out to the edges, without going over. Again, pureé should be no more than $1/4$-inch thick.

Place trays inside dehydrator, open vents, and turn on. Total drying time varies with the type ofdehydrator, thickness of the leather, and juiciness of the fruit. If you desire a thicker leather, simply spread another thin layer of pureé on top of the already dried sheets and dry once again. Fruit leathers will store nicely in the refrigerator for a couple of months.

Breads & Breakfasts

BREADS

The well-known camper's bannock bread or flat bread is the modern day equivalent of the johnnycake. "Johnnycake" was a fried, flat bread popular in Colonial America. (The origin of the word apparently came from the term "journey cake," since the bread was easily transported and kept well on long journeys. It could even be made along the way.) It has become a staple for backpackers who want a dish to round out a meal of camp stew or chili.

Bannock Bread

    1 cup flour
    $^1/_4$ tsp salt
    2 Tbsp powdered milk
    1 tsp baking powder

Combine ingredients before your camping trip and store in a zip-lock bag. Just before cooking, add water to make a stiff dough. Spoon batter into a lightly greased frying pan; cover. Cook over medium to low coals, turning when browned on the first side. Continue cooking until bread is done all the way through.

Basic Pocketbread

    $1^1/_2$ cups whole wheat flour
    $^1/_2$ cup water
    1 Tbsp vegetable oil

Combine flour and oil. Add water, a little at a time, until a soft dough forms. Knead on a floured surface for 10 minutes. Divide the dough into 6 parts. Roll each part into a ball and flatten into a 6-inch circle. Fry on an ungreased griddle over medium hot coals for about 30-45 seconds. Bubbles will form as it cooks. Turn and fry the other side. (To encourage the formation of a pocket, press down on the bread as soon as it is turned.) Serve hot or wrap in plastic wrap for later use.

Breadsticks Italiano

Quick and easy to make. These just take a few minutes of cooking over medium to low coals.

> **7-oz tube of soft breadstick dough**
> **Butter**
> **Garlic powder or garlic bread sprinkle**

Cut one foot lengths of green sticks. Scrub with water and dry. Unroll the tube of breadsticks and separate. Wrap one breadstick around each stick. (Edges of dough should touch each other but not overlap. See illustration.) Brush a little salad oil on a cooking grate and place over medium-low coals, or suspend the breadsticks above the grate.

Grill shish kabob fashion for 6-8 minutes, turning frequently to prevent burning. Remove from heat when bread is a golden brown. Brush breadsticks with butter and sprinkle on garlic. Gently push the bread off the stick. Serve immediately. Makes 4 servings.

Chapatis

1 cup flour (may be a combination)
Pinch of salt
Vegetable oil
$^1/_4$-$^1/_3$ cup water

Combine flour and salt. Add 1 Tablespoon of oil, stirring slowly to blend. Add water, a little at a time, until a slightly sticky dough forms.

Turn dough out onto a slightly oiled work surface. Knead for 10 minutes, or until dough is smooth. Cover with plastic wrap and rest for 20-30 minutes.

Divide dough into 6 equal parts. Roll each part into a ball and flatten into a 6-inch circle. Fry on an ungreased griddle over medium-hot coals for 30 seconds on one side. Turn, and fry the other side. Lift with a spatula occasionally to keep from sticking. The bread should puff up.

China Rolls

1 bunch green onions
7.5-oz container buttermilk biscuit dough
Flour
Soy sauce or sesame oil
Vegetable oil

Finely chop green onions; set aside. Separate dough into 10 individual biscuits. On a floured surface, roll each biscuit into a thin circle. Brush the tops of each with soy sauce or a few drops of sesame oil; top with onions.

Roll up each circle, jelly roll fashion. Fashion the biscuit into a knot, by tucking ends under. Then, roll each knot into a flat circle.

Heat oil in a heavy skillet over medium-hot coals. Fry in hot oil until golden brown on one side. Turn and fry the other side. Remove from oil and drain. Serve immediately. Makes 10 China Rolls.

Cinnamon Doughboys

1 tube refrigerated biscuit dough
Melted butter
Cinnamon and sugar

Separate dough into 8 pieces. Roll each piece between your hands until it is long and thin. Wrap the dough around a stick, pulling it as you go to make it thinner. Brush with melted butter. Roll in cinnamon and sugar. Toast over hot coals. Yummy!

French Bread in Foil

1 loaf French bread
$^3/_4$ cup melted butter
3 tablespoons dry onion powder

Cut bread diagonally at 1-inch intervals, but do not cut all the way through. Combine onion powder and melted butter. Brush lightly between the slices and on the top of the bread. Wrap securely in heavy-duty aluminum foil (or double thickness of regular foil) and heat on the grill or in a reflector oven.

Variation: Garlic/Cheese Bread
Substitute 1 loaf of frozen garlic or cheese bread for the French bread. Omit extra butter and onion powder. Wrap in aluminum foil and heat on the grill or in a reflector oven. For best results, thaw bread before heating.

Mandarin Pancakes

2 cups flour
1 cup boiling water
Peanut oil or sesame oil

Combine flour and water until a soft dough forms. Transfer to a floured surface and knead until smooth, about 5 minutes. Divide the dough into 8 sections. Cut each section in half.

Working with two pieces at a time, roll each piece into a 5-inch circle. Brush the top of one circle with a few drops of peanut oil (or sesame oil for a spicier pancake). Top with the other circle. Roll each double circle into one 8-inch circle.

Fry each double circle on an ungreased griddle over medium coals. Turn frequently until air bubbles appear on the surface and the pancake is dry to the touch. Repeat with remaining dough. Fill with your choice of stir-fried meats and vegetables and enjoy.

Sopaipillas

$1\frac{1}{4}$ cup warm water
1 pkg active dry yeast
2 tsp sugar
1 Tbsp butter, melted
1 beaten egg or $\frac{1}{4}$ cup egg substitute
$3-3\frac{1}{4}$ cups flour
Oil for deep frying
Honey

Dissolve yeast in warm water. Add the sugar, butter, and egg; mix well. Add the flour, $\frac{1}{2}$ cup at a time, until you have a soft, pliable dough. Turn onto a floured surface and knead the dough for five minutes. Cover, and let rise until double, about 20-30 minutes.

Roll out dough to a ¹/₄-inch thickness and cut into 2-inch squares. Heat oil in a large frying pan over medium-hot coals. Carefully drop dough into hot oil and fry in small batches until brown on one side. Turn and brown the other side. Drain on paper towels. Serve warm with honey. Or, omit honey, and roll in a mixture of cinnamon and sugar. Serve immediately after cooking. These "little pillows" will loose some of their taste the next day.

Variation: French Beignets

Using the recipe above, add 1¹/₂ tsp. vanilla extract to the sugar, butter, and egg mixture. Prepare dough as in Sopaipillas. Fry in hot oil until golden brown. Drain on paper towels. Roll in powdered sugar.

Stick Bread

1 cup Bisquick®
¹/₄ cup water

Remove the bark from a few green sticks. Wash and pat dry.

Combine Bisquick® and water. Stir until a soft dough forms. Wrap a small amount of the dough around one end of the stick. Grill over low coals for about 15 minutes, turning often.

Warming Bread and Rolls

Place bread, rolls, or muffins on an aluminum pie plate. Invert another pie plate on top. Rest 5 minutes on top of a pot of boiling water for warm, delicious bread. Remember, the pie pan will be HOT.

BREAKFASTS

Butters

Banana Nut Butter

$^1/_2$ cup butter, softened
1 ripe banana, mashed
$^1/_4$ cup finely chopped nuts

Cream the butter. Stir in the banana and nuts, and blend well. Cover and chill until ready for use.

Honey Butter

$^1/_2$ cup butter
$^1/_2$ cup honey

Combine butter and honey. Blend thoroughly. Serve on toast or pancakes. Chill any remaining honey butter.

Syrups

Blackberry Syrup

1 cup fresh blackberries or raspberries
$^1/_2$ cup sugar
Water

Cook berries and sugar in a saucepan over medium-hot coals, stirring constantly and crushing berries. Add a small amount of water and mix well. Boil for 1 minute. The blackberry mixture should be the consistency of syrup. Adjust water as necessary.

Cherry Syrup

Wisconsin Regional Cherry Growers Association

1 cup cherry juice
1 cup white sugar
1 cup white corn syrup

Combine all ingredients. Bring to a boil, then move away from direct heat and simmer for 15 minutes. Great over pancakes and French toast.

Maple Syrup

Maple syrup production is a vital part of the local economy in dozens of communities from Maine westward into Minnesota, and south to Indiana and West Virginia.

There are thirteen species of maples native to the United States. Only the sugar maple and black sugar maple are of importance in the production of maple syrup, because of the sweetness of their sap. Other species of maples commonly found in hardwood forests, such as the red maple and the silver maple, are not good sources of maple syrup. Their sap is less sweet than the sugar maple and often contains excessive amounts of sugar sand. Maple trees can be readily identified by their leaves (illustrated below).

Black Maple Sugar Maple

Red Maple Silver Maple

Maple sap begins to flow late in March or early April, when the days are warm and sunny and the nights are cool. A small hole is bored into the trunk of the tree and a plastic or metal spout is inserted. A bucket placed underneath the spout collects the sap. Then the sap is boiled down, filtered, and packed into containers.

Most commercial brands of pancake syrup contain less than 2% pure maple syrup. But maple syrup doesn't just have to be served at breakfast. It will perk up the flavor of many recipes. Try it for unique tasting beverages, desserts, and vegetables. Use it in a basting sauce for meats, and add it as an extra sweetener in your fruit dips. Be creative—the uses are endless.

Pure maple syrup may also replace granualted sugar in many recipes. To substitute maple syrup for sugar, use $1^1/_2$ cups of maple syrup for each cup of granulated sugar, then add $^1/_4$ teaspoon of baking soda for each cup of maple syrup used. When maple syrup is substituted for all sugar in a recipe, decrease liquid by one-half.

Cereal
Crunchy Granola

$^1/_2$ **cup vegetable oil**
$^1/_2$ **to 1 cup honey**
1 Tbsp vanilla
4 Tbsp powdered milk
1 cup wheat germ
$1^1/_4$ cup sesame seeds
$^1/_2$ to 2 cups shredded coconut
7 cups rolled oats

Combine oil, honey, and vanilla in a large saucepan. Heat over medium heat until mixture is runny. Stir in remaining ingredients, coating with honey mixture. Spread in a thin layer on a baking sheet. Bake in a 225° F oven for 1½ hours, or until lightly browned. Cool and store in an air-tight container.

To serve, place in a bowl and add fresh cold milk.

Easy Campers Breakfast

Make as soon as you get up in the morning and a warm breakfast will be waiting for you by the time you are dressed.

Instant oatmeal
Raisins or nuts
Boiling water

Fill your thermos half-full with oatmeal, and add raisins or nuts. Pour boiling water over all, leaving 1 inch of headspace at the top. Close your thermos and wait at least 30-45 minutes.

Variation: Stewed Fruit (Make the night before serving.)
Warm, stewed fruit can also be made in a thermos. In a saucepan, heat approximately 2 oz of dried fruit and water to boiling. Boil for two minutes, then transfer to your thermos, adding enough hot water to cover. Close thermos and wait until morning.

Maple Granola

4 cups rolled oats
1 cup unsalted peanuts
½ cup oat bran
½ cup vegetable oil
½ tsp Lite® salt
½ cup sesame seeds
½ cup pure maple syrup
½ cup raisins
1 cup coconut

Combine dry ingredients. Mix in oil and syrup. Spread in a jelly roll pan and bake at 325° F for 25 minutes, stirring several times. In the last 5 minutes, add raisins and coconut.

Eggs

Baked Eggs

6 large eggs
Butter
Salt and pepper to taste

Butter six disposable aluminum muffin cups. Break an egg into each one. Bake 12-15 minutes in reflector oven. Position the oven further away from the flames if the eggs are cooking too quickly. Season with salt and pepper to taste. Makes 6 hot servings.

Soft and Hard Cooked Eggs

Eggs can cook over the campfire in a pan, or even in a non-waxed paper cup. Set the eggs in a pan and cover with water. If using a paper cup, place one egg per cup and add enough cold water to cover. The water prevents the cup from burning. Position the pan or cup on hot coals and bring the water to a boil. Remove from heat. Cover and let rest for:

| Soft cooked | 5-8 minutes |
| Hard cooked | 20 minutes |

Immerse eggs in cold water to prevent further cooking.

Eggs and Muffins a L' Orange

4 large navel oranges
1 pkg (7 oz) bran muffin mix
4 eggs
Salt and pepper

Cut oranges in half horizontally. Remove fruit, keeping peels intact. If peels are thick, you can remove the fruit by sliding your finger or a spoon all the way around the orange until the fruit may be removed easily.

Prepare muffin mix according to package directions. Fill one orange-peel "cup" $^2/_3$ full with muffin batter. Break an egg into the other. Lay each filled cup in the center of a 10-inch square of heavy duty aluminum foil. Bring the sides of the foil together around the cups. Gather foil together above the food and twist, leaving enough space above muffin batter for the muffins to rise.

Nestle on hot coals and cook 10-15 minutes. Remove from coals and serve with orange slices or juice.

Eggs and Mushrooms

Butter
Fresh mushrooms, cleaned and sliced
Eggs, well-beaten
Milk

Melt a small amount of butter in a heavy skillet over medium coals. Add mushrooms, saute until tender. Combine eggs and milk. You will need approximately 1 tablespoon of milk per egg. Pour over mushrooms in the skillet. Scramble together until eggs are done. Season with salt and pepper to taste.

Eggs and Potatoes

For each person have:

1 medium baking potato, scrubbed
1 egg
Butter

Butter the outside of the potato, wrap in foil, and bake in hot coals until done. Remove from heat. Slice open the potato, but don't cut all the way through. Open the potato slightly, place a pat of butter inside. Break an egg into the potato, rewrap in aluminum foil, and return to the coals, egg side up. Bake until the egg is set. Season with salt and pepper to taste.

Egg-in-a-Hole

Eggs
Bread
Butter or margarine

Butter both sides of a slice of bread. Cut a hole in the center. Place the buttered bread in a skillet over medium-hot coals. Crack an egg into the hole and cook until half done. Carefully turn the bread and egg over and cook the other side until the egg is completely done. Cook any leftover pieces of bread.

French Toast
Peanut Butter French Toast

Bread
Peanut butter
Butter or margarine
Eggs
Milk
Sugar

Make a peanut butter sandwich for each camper. Beat an egg, 1 teaspoon of sugar, and a small amount of milk together to make a batter. Melt 1-2 tablespoons of butter in a skillet over medium-hot coals. Dip each sandwich in the batter and fry until golden brown on both sides. Serve with maple syrup or jelly of your choice.

Fruit
Apple Fritters

1 cup prepared pancake batter
2 large firm apples
Sugar
Cinnamon

Combine cinnamon and sugar in a bowl; set aside.

Peel and core apples and cut into wedges. Dip each wedge into the prepared pancake batter. Fry in hot oil until golden brown. Drain on paper towels. While still warm, roll the fritters in the cinnamon-sugar mixture.

Applesauce Pancakes

6 cups flour
2 tsp salt
2 tsp baking powder
1 tsp cinnamon
1 quart applesauce, unsweetened
$1/4$ cup cooking oil
6 Tbsp maple syrup or sugar
2 eggs, well-beaten
Water or milk

Combine flour, salt, baking powder, and cinnamon. Blend in applesauce, syrup or sugar, oil, and eggs. Stir in enough water or milk until the batter becomes easy to pour. Bake in a heavy skillet over medium-hot coals until pancakes are golden brown on both sides.

Variation: Applesauce Crepes
Following the above recipe, create a thin batter by adding a little more water or milk. Fry as directed, roll, and dust with powdered sugar.

Baked Apples Granola

For each person have:
1 large firm apple
3 Tbsp granola cereal
1 tsp butter
1 tsp brown sugar
Dash of cinnamon

Core apple, but don't cut all the way through. Combine granola, brown sugar, and cinnamon. Stuff the granola mixture inside the apple; dot with butter. Wrap the apple in a double thickness of aluminum foil. Place on medium-hot coals and cook for 20 minutes. Cool slightly before serving. Makes one serving.

Chunky Applesauce

5 lbs cooking apples
1 cup water
1$^1/_2$ cup sugar

Peel, core, and cut apples into large chunks. Place in a large heavy skillet. Stir in water and sugar. Cover tightly, and cook over medium coals for 5 minutes, stirring occasionally and adding a little more water if necessary. Uncover and cook 5 minutes more, or until apples are tender. Some chunks will remain. Serve warm. Makes about 2 quarts.

Variation: For additional flavor, add cinnamon or maple syrup to taste. It's delicious either way.

Maple Baked Apples

For each person have:
    Firm, ripe baking apple
    Pure maple syrup

Core apple about one-third of the way down. Fill the cavity with maple syrup. Place the apple on a double thickness of aluminum foil. Bring foil up around sides, twist top, and cook over medium-hot coals for 20 minutes.

Maple Baked Bananas

6 firm bananas
2 Tbsp lemon juice
$^3/_4$ cup pure maple syrup
$^1/_3$ cup chopped peanuts

Peel bananas. Brush with lemon juice and arrange in a greased aluminum baking dish. Pour maple syrup over bananas and bake in a reflector oven with moderate heat for 15 minutes, rotating occasionally. Carefully remove from oven, place on individual plates and sprinkle with chopped peanuts. Serves 6.

Variation: Coconut Baked Bananas

Omit maple syrup and nuts. Peel bananas, brush with lemon juice or pineapple juice, and roll in flaked coconut. Arrange in a greased aluminum baking dish. Bake as directed above, rotating occasionally. Serves 6.

Orange Fritters

1 cup prepared pancake batter
1 tsp grated orange rind
2 oranges

Peel and separate two oranges into sections. Remove seeds carefully, keeping orange sections intact.

Combine grated orange rind and prepared pancake batter. Dip each orange section into the batter and fry in hot oil until golden brown. Drain on paper towels. Serve with orange sauce.

Orange Sauce: Beat 3 ounces of softened cream cheese until smooth. Add 3 Tbsp orange juice (or prepared Tang® orange drink.) Beat again till smooth.

Stewed Fruit

*See **Easy Camper's Breakfast**, on p. 51.*

Meats
Breakfast Kabobs

1 pkg Brown and Serve® sausage links
1 can pineapple chunks
2 medium oranges, cut into wedges
2 medium potatoes, cut into ¼-inch thick slices
1 green bell pepper, seeded and cut into squares
Fruit preserves (pineapple, orange, or whatever)

Alternate first five ingredients onto wooden or metal skewers. Grill over hot coals, basting with preserves and turning occasionally for 10-12 minutes, or until sausages are thoroughly cooked and vegetables are tender. Warm remaining preserves. Serve with kabobs. Makes 4 servings.

Campfire Muffins

4 English muffins, split
4 slices Monterey Jack cheese
4 slices cooked ham
¼ cup pineapple preserves

Split muffins and arrange on a baking sheet or aluminum foil pan. Place a cheese and ham slice on the bottom half of the muffins. Brush the inside of the muffin tops with pineapple preserves. Place in the reflector oven and bake for 5-7 minutes, roatating occasionally, until cheese is melted and ham is heated through. Carefully remove from oven and press muffin halves together to serve. Makes 4 campfire muffins.

Campfire Steak and Eggs

Butter
Breakfast or sandwich steaks
Eggs

Melt 1 Tbsp butter in a heavy skillet over medium coals. Brown steaks on one side, then turn. Break the eggs over the steak. Cover the skillet, and cook slowly until eggs are done.

Sausages N' Apples

6 large baking apples
6 breakfast link sausages

Core apples and insert one sausage link in the center. Wrap each apple in a double thickness of aluminum foil. Bake in hot coals for 30-40 minutes. Serve right from the foil. Makes 6 baked apples.

Stick Bacon

Clean a green stick and sharpen one end. Make a hole in one end of a strip of bacon and push onto the stick. Wrap the bacon around the stick and poke the end of the stick through the other end of the bacon. Cook over hot coals, turning frequently, until the bacon is crisp.

Light Fare

Salads
Soups and Stews
Sandwiches

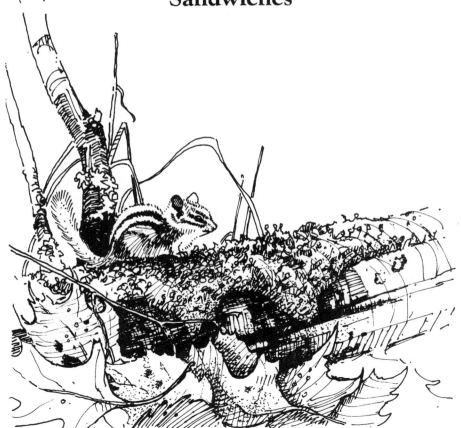

SALADS

1-2-3 Salad

1 onion, diced
2 dill pickles, diced
3 apples, peeled, cored, and diced
Salad dressing

Combine onion, pickles, and apples in a mixing bowl. Add enough salad dressing to moisten. Serve cold.

Backpacker's Salad

3 oz cream cheese
$\frac{1}{2}$ cup chopped nuts
$\frac{1}{2}$ teaspoon cinnamon
1 Tbsp sugar
4 large apples

Combine first four ingredients in a small bowl; set aside. Cut the tops from the apples. Core carefully so you do not cut through to the bottom of the apples. Fill each apple with the cream cheese mixture. Replace the tops of the apples. Wrap in foil to keep crisp. Makes 4 salads.

Banana Fruit Salad

1 large banana, cut into $\frac{1}{2}$-inch slices
1 can pineapple tidbits in juice
1 large apple, diced

1 small can mandarin oranges, drained
1 chopped pecans or walnuts
1 cup light mayonnaise

Drain pineapple, reserving juice. Combine fruit and nuts in a medium bowl; set aside. In a small bowl, beat mayonnaise until creamy. Add a small amount of reserved pineapple juice to thin mayonnaise; pour over fruit. Chill and serve. Serves four.

Cattail Salad

Harvest cattails very early in the spring when they are just be-ginning to send up new shoots. Cut off the small shoots that are between 1 and $2^{1}/_{2}$ inches long. Clean thoroughly so only the solid white part remains. Coarsely chop, add salt, and your fa-vorite salad dressing to taste.

CAUTION: Do not pick cattails from an area where pollutants or urban run-off may be present.

Cole Slaw

1 cup light mayonnaise or salad dressing
2 Tbsp milk
1 Tbsp sugar
$^1/_2$ tsp celery seed
3 cups finely shredded cabbage
2 carrots, finely shredded

Combine the first four ingredients to make the salad dressing. Place the cabbage and carrots in a large bowl. Pour dressing on top and toss to coat. Serve chilled. Serves four.

Variation: Omit carrots, add 1 small finely chopped onion and 1 green pepper, thinly sliced.

Fiesta Salad

1 cup mayonnaise
1 Tbsp chili powder
1 tsp catsup or chili sauce
Dash of cayenne pepper
Salt and pepper to taste
16-oz can kidney beans
1 cucumber, diced
1 small onion, finely chopped
1 green pepper, diced
3 large tomatoes, diced
4 slices bacon, cooked and crumbled

Combine mayonnaise and seasonings in a large bowl. Drain beans and vegetables. Mix all ingredients together, except bacon, and chill. Add bacon just before serving. Serves 6-8.

Lemon Pork Salad

For Sodium Restricted Diets

$^1/_3$ cup cooked trimmed pork loin,
  cut into thin strips
1 medium carrot, diagonally sliced
$^1/_2$ cup red or green seedless grapes
1 cup torn fresh spinach
2 Tbsp lemon-flavored yogurt

Combine pork strips, carrots, and grapes. Place spinach in a container with a tight fitting lid. Top with pork mixture. Chill for several hours. Before serving, spoon on yogurt. Makes 1 serving.

Marinated Vegetable Salad

$^1/_4$ cup white wine vinegar
2 Tbsp water
.6-oz pkg Zesty Italian® salad dressing mix
$^1/_2$ cup salad oil
1 cup broccoli flowerets
1 cup cauliflower flowerets
1 cup carrot sticks, cut into 2-inch pieces

Combine vinegar and water in a jar with lid. Add salad dressing mix and salad oil; shake vigorously. (This may be prepared prior to your camping trip and kept refrigerated.) Wash vegetables and cut into bite sized pieces. (Vegetables can also be prepared in advance and carried to the campsite in a large zip lock plastic bag.)

Pour salad dressing over vegetables in zip lock bag; shake to coat. Marinate in the refrigerator or cooler for 2-3 hours, shaking several times. If desired, garnish salad with grated Parmesan cheese before serving. Makes 2-3 servings.

Pork Salad

2 cups roast pork
1 cup celery
1 onion
$^1/_2$ red pepper
Mayonnaise or salad dressing

Dice the roast pork. Coarsely chop celery, onion, and pepper. Combine with pork in a medium bowl. Add enough mayonnaise to moisten. Serve on lettuce leaves. Makes 4 servings.

Pudding Salad

Assorted fresh or canned fruits (bananas, strawberries, apples, pineapple or whatever is available)
Instant vanilla pudding

Cut up fresh fruit into large chunks. If using canned fruit, drain off most of the juice. Place the fruit in a medium bowl and sprinkle on a little instant pudding powder. Toss gently to coat; set aside for 10 minutes. For a thicker dressing, add more pudding mix, for a thinner dressing, add more water.

Quick and Easy Cole Slaw

16-oz jar sweet pickle relish
$2^1/_2$ cups shredded cabbage
1 cup shredded carrots

Combine all ingredients, mixing well. Chill for several hours, allowing flavors to blend. Makes 6 servings.

Tomato-Basil Salad

4 medium tomatoes
1 small red onion
2 tsp dried basil
$^1/_4$-$^1/_3$ cup red wine vinegar
Pepper to taste

Thinly slice tomatoes and onion. Toss with basil. Pour wine vinegar over the salad, add pepper if desired; toss to coat. Marinate for at least one-half hour, but preferably 1-2 hours. Add more pepper to taste when serving. Serves 4-5.

Waldorf Salad

Salad:
  1 Golden Delicious apple, chopped
  1 Granny Smith apple, chopped
  1 large MacIntosh apple, chopped
  1 stalk celery, chopped
  $^1/_2$ cup chopped walnuts

Dressing:
  $^1/_2$ cup light mayonnaise
  1 Tbsp sugar
  Dash of salt

In a medium bowl combine apples, celery and walnuts. In a small bowl combine dressing ingredients. Pour dressing over the salad; stir gently to coat. Chill, and serve over a bed of greens. Or, if desired, cut a tomato in half. Scoop out the seeds and spoon $^3/_4$ cup of salad into each half. Makes a very attractive salad, and the salad "bowl" is edible.

Walking Salad

4 large apples
$^1\!/_2$ cup chunky peanut butter
$^1\!/_4$ cup raisins

Combine peanut butter and raisins; set aside. Cut the tops from the apples. Core carefully so you do not cut through to the bottom of the apples. Fill the cavity of each with the peanut butter/raisin mixture. Replace the tops of the apples. Wrap securely in aluminum foil to keep apples crisp and fresh.

Backpacking Fresh Vegetables

Vegetable	How to Prepare
Broccoli	Wash; cut into florets. Wrap in a wet paper towel and foil.
Carrots	Scrub clean; do not peel.
Cauliflower	Wash; cut into florets. Wrap in a wet paper towel and foil.
Celery	Wash; cut into sticks. Wrap in a wet paper towel and foil.
Cucumber	Wash; leave whole. Slice only when ready to eat. Smaller cucumbers are easier to carry and contain less seeds.
Green Beans	Wash; do not cut. Wrap in foil.
Onions	Leave whole; do not peel.
Peas/Snow Peas	Wash pods; do not shuck peas.

Watermelon Basket Salad

Always a crowd-pleaser, especially at family reunions and picnics.

1 large watermelon
1 honeydew melon
2 musk melons
2 pints fresh strawberries
1 pint bing cherries
1 small pineapple, cut into chunks

Wash and dry watermelon. Using a sharp knife, cut the watermelon in half lengthwise, leaving a 1-inch strip in the middle for the "handle" of the basket. (See illustration.)

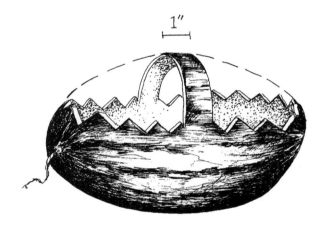

Cut along dotted lines.

Scoop out the inside of the melon, reserving fruit. Cut reserved watermelon into chunks; set aside. Cut the fruit of the other melons into chunks; set aside. Clean and hull strawberries. Combine fruits and arrange in the basket. Reserve leftover fruit for second helpings.

Serve with **Marshmallow-Cream Cheese Dressing** (p. 144)

SOUPS and STEWS

Brunswick Stew

4-5 lb stewing chicken, quartered
1 medium onion, sliced
2 strips bacon, diced
6 cups hot water
28-oz can tomatoes
1 can kernel corn
1 can lima beans
3 medium potatoes, sliced or 1 can whole
1 can small potatoes
Salt and pepper to taste

Arrange chicken quarters in the bottom of a Dutch oven. Add onion and bacon; cover with hot water. Cook on a grate over a medium fire, or suspend Dutch oven from a tripod over the fire, until meat is tender, about 1 hour. Remove chicken from stew, bone out, and cut into bite-sized pieces. Return meat to stew and add remaining ingredients. Cook until potatoes are tender.

Camp Chowder

1 can cream of celery soup
1 can cream of potato soup
1$\frac{1}{2}$ cups canned vegetables
2 Tbsp onion flakes
2 cups milk (reconstituted from powder)
$\frac{3}{4}$-1 lb ham (or hot dogs), cut into chunks

Combine all ingredients and heat thoroughly. Serve with bread or crackers.

Camper's Seafood Gumbo

2 cans (10 oz) chicken and rice soup
10 oz frozen cut okra
16 oz stewed tomatoes
6-oz can shrimp, rinsed and drained
6 oz crab, rinsed and drained
$1/4$ tsp garlic powder
Tabasco sauce, season to taste

Prepare soup as directed in a Dutch oven, then add all other ingredients. Cook slowly over medium-low coals for 30 minutes. Taste for seasonings and adjust accordingly.

Campfire Stew

2 lb hamburger or 4 cups leftover meat
2 onions, sliced
6 Tbsp cooking oil
1 cup macaroni, cooked
3 15-oz cans kidney beans
2 cans (1 lb each) tomatoes
Salt and pepper to taste

Heat oil in a heavy skillet over medium-hot coals. Brown onions and meat, and drain off fat. Combine all remaining ingredients, adding as much water as desired. Salt and pepper to taste. Simmer 20 minutes and serve.

Chicken Booyah

2 lb beef, cut into 1-inch cubes
1 gallon water
3 lb stewing chicken, cut up
1 cup cabbage, chopped
2 medium onions, chopped
$\frac{1}{2}$ tsp nutmeg
$10\frac{1}{2}$-oz can tomato soup
2 cups celery, chopped
3 cups carrots, sliced
3 cups potatoes, peeled and cubed
1 lb can of peas
1 Tbsp salt
$\frac{1}{2}$ tsp pepper

Brown beef in a large kettle over an open fire. Either place kettle on a grate over the fire or suspend from a tripod over the fire. Cover with one gallon water; cook for 30 minutes. Add chicken; cook for 1 hour. Add cabbage, onions, nutmeg, and tomato soup; cook for 45 minutes. Add the celery; cook for an additional 30 minutes. Then add the carrots; cook for 30 minutes. Add the potatoes; cook for 30 minutes. Finally add the peas, salt and pepper. Cook for 30 minutes. Feeds a hungry crowd.

Delicious Fish Chowder

$2\frac{1}{2}$ lbs potatoes
1 large onion, diced
1 Tbsp salt
2 lbs fresh fish fillets
14-oz can whole tomatoes
$\frac{1}{2}$ pint half-and-half cream
1 stick butter

$^3/_4$ **tsp pepper**
$^1/_8$ **lb soda crackers**

Quarter, and thinly slice, potatoes. Rinse well with cold water to remove excess starch; drain. Place in a large fish kettle over hot coals. Add diced onion and salt. Cover with water and boil until potatoes are tender. Break potatoes into small chunks.

Add 2 pounds of cubed, skinned and boned fish fillets. (You may use fillets from a variety of fish.) Slowly bring to another boil. Cook until fish flakes easily. Remove from heat. Add tomatoes, half-and-half, butter, pepper, and crumpled soda crackers; mix well. Wait 5 minutes before serving.

Note: Total mixture will be about $1^1/_2$ gallons, so start with a large kettle. If you like a little tang, add 6 strips of crisply fried bacon, diced.

Easy Camp Stew

Vegetable oil
Beef roast
Canned tomatoes
Cream of mushroom soup
Onions
Carrots
Potatoes
Water

Establish a good bed of coals. Heat 1-2 Tbsp oil in a Dutch oven, then add meat. After the meat is browned, fill the Dutch oven with canned tomatoes, cream of mushroom soup, onion, carrots, potatoes, or whatever you like. Cover, and set in coals, or just above, for $1^1/_2$ to 2 hours. Make sure you have enough water or liquid while cooking to prevent burning. Serve hot.

Fish Chowder

1 lb lean fish
2$\frac{1}{2}$ cups water
2 cups raw potatoes, cubed
4 strips bacon, fried crisp
2 Tbsp flour
$\frac{1}{4}$-$\frac{1}{2}$ cup onions, sliced
3 cups hot milk

Heat water in a Dutch oven over medium-hot coals. Add fish; simmer for 15 minutes or until fish is tender. Drain, saving stock. Remove skin and bones, then flake the fish and set aside.

Add potatoes to the stock, cook until tender. Add the onions and bacon; cook 3-5 minutes. Stir in flour until mixture is slightly thickened. Finally, add the fish and milk. Bring just to the boiling point. Serve immediately. Makes 6 servings.

Heather's Corn Chowder

5 slices bacon, fried crisp and crumbled
1 can cream of potato soup
16-oz can whole kernel corn, drained
1 tsp instant onion
$\frac{3}{4}$ cup milk
Salt and pepper to taste

Combine all ingredients in a pot and heat slowly. Simmer for 10 minutes to heat through. Add more milk or water for a thinner soup. Serve hot with crackers or slices of French bread.

Note: Powdered milk works very well in this recipe. It's less expensive and is easily stored.

Savory Cheese Soup

$^1/_4$ cup butter
$^1/_4$ cup flour
1 cup milk
1 8-oz tub Sharp Cheddar Cold Pack Cheese®
1 large can mixed vegetables
$10^3/_4$ oz can chicken broth

Melt butter in a saucepan over medium coals. Blend in flour until smooth. Gradually add milk, stirring constantly until thickened. Stir in the cheese, blending well until smooth. Drain vegetables and add to cheese mixture. Add chicken broth, stirring once again until smooth. Warm gently. Makes 4-6 servings.

Wild Rice Mushroom Soup

$^1/_3$ cup butter or margarine
1 large onion, finely chopped
$^1/_3$ cup flour
Salt and pepper
2 cans undiluted chicken broth
16 oz fresh mushrooms, thinly sliced
2 cups half-and-half
2 cups cooked wild rice

Melt butter in Dutch oven over medium coals. Stir in onion and cook until tender. Season flour with salt and pepper to taste. Sprinkle over onions, then stir constantly until mixture thickens. Gradually stir in chicken broth. Continue stirring until mixture begins to thicken. Add remaining ingredients. Stir slowly for 10-15 minutes to heat through.

SANDWICHES

Bratwurst

Grilled Bratwurst

2 lbs uncooked bratwurst
2 large onions, sliced
2 cans beer

Grill bratwurst over hot coals until brown on all sides. Remove from grill. Place in a large kettle, cover with beer, and add onions. Simmer 1 hour. (Heating removes the alcohol content of the beer.) Brats may be left simmering for several hours, if desired. Serve hot on brat buns with desired toppings. Serves 6.

Burgers

Grilled Hamburgers

2 lbs lean ground beef
8 hamburger buns

Divide ground beef into 8 portions. Shape each portion into a ball, then flatten into a patty. Grill burgers over medium coals for 8-10 minutes, turning halfway through cooking time. Serve on hamburger buns with desired toppings. Serves 8.

Best-Ever BBQ'S

2 lbs ground chuck
1 egg, beaten
Barbecue sauce
$^1/_4$ cup shredded cheddar cheese
$^1/_4$ cup finely chopped onion
$^1/_4$ cup pickle relish
8 hamburger buns

Combine ground chuck, egg, and $^1/_4$ cup barbecue sauce; mix thoroughly. Shape into 16 round, thin patties. Place 1 teaspoon each of cheese, onion, pickle relish, and barbecue sauce on half of the patties. Top each with a remaining patty, sealing edges well. Grill on foil over hot coals until done, turning once gently. Burgers are very juicy and delicious. Serve on hamburger buns. Serves 8.

Chili Burgers

1 lb ground beef
$^1/_2$ large green pepper, chopped
1 small onion, chopped
1 Tbsp chili sauce
1 Tbsp chili powder
Salt and pepper to taste

Combine all ingredients, mixing well. Shape into patties. Grill as you would hamburgers. Serve hot on buns with catsup or extra chili sauce.

Hot Dogs

Grilled Hot Dogs

Frankfurters
Hot dog buns

Grill over medium-hot coals, turning occasionally, for 6-8 minutes. Serve on hot dog buns with desired toppings.

Barbecued Hot Dogs

$^2/_3$ **cup steak sauce**
$^1/_2$ **cup pineapple preserves**
2 Tbsp butter
1 Tbsp brown sugar
Hot dogs

Combine first four ingredients. Heat in a small saucepan over low coals until sugar dissolves, stirring occasionally. Grill hot dogs over hot coals, basting with sauce. Turn frequently.

Cheesy Hot Dogs

4 hot dogs
Cheddar cheese
4 strips of bacon
4 hot dog buns

Split hot dogs in half, lengthwise; insert a thin strip of cheese. Wrap with a strip of bacon and secure with a wooden toothpick. Grill over hot coals until bacon cooks to desired doneness. Serve on hot dog buns. Serves 4.

Suggested Toppings for Burgers and Hot Dogs	
catsup	chili
pickles, relish	barbecue sauce
cheese	onions, thinly sliced
minced tomatoes	minced green peppers
mustard	bottled salsa dressing

Other Sandwiches
Bacon and Egg Sandwiches

6 hard-boiled eggs, chopped
6 strips bacon, fried crisp and crumbled
3 oz cream cheese with chives
2 Tbsp salad dressing

Combine all ingredients and mix thoroughly; chill. Serve on bread or hard rolls.

Beef Krautwich Hero

3 pkg (3 oz each) cream cheese
2 Tbsp milk
2 Tbsp chopped chives
16-oz can sauerkraut, well drained
18 slices pumpernickel bread
(about one medium loaf)
Butter, softened
6 oz sliced smoked beef

Blend 3 oz cream cheese, milk, and 1 Tbsp chives. Stir in sauerkraut and chill. In a medium bowl, blend remaining cream cheese and chives.

Using 3 slices of bread for each sandwich, assemble as follows: On the first slice, spread ¹/₃ cup of the sauerkraut mixture. On the second slice, spread 2 Tbsp of the cheese mixture and add several slices of beef. Butter remaining slice and top sandwich. Makes 6 sandwiches.

Deviled Ham and Egg Sandwich

3-oz pkg cream cheese with chives
¹/₄ cup salad dressing
1 can deviled ham
1 tsp prepared mustard
6 hard-cooked eggs, coarsely chopped

Combine cream cheese, salad dressing, ham, and mustard. Mix well. Stir in eggs. Chill at least one hour to blend flavors. Spread on toast or bread. Makes about 1 cup spread.

Fish and Kraut Sandwiches

1 cup cooked, flaked fish
¹/₂ cup well drained sauerkraut
¹/₄ cup chopped dill pickles
¹/₄ cup mayonnaise
1 Tbsp horseradish
12 slices party rye bread
4 slices (1 oz each) Swiss cheese
2 Tbsp butter

Combine fish, sauerkraut, pickles, mayonnaise, and horserad-ish; mix well. Portion mixture evenly on half the bread. Top with cheese and remaining bread.

Melt margarine in a skillet over medium-low coals. Place sand-wiches in the skillet and grill on each side until golden brown. Serve with chips or relishes and a cold drink. Makes 4 servings.

Gyros

1 lb ground lamb, beef, or combination
2 Tbsp garlic salt
1 small onion, thinly sliced
1 cup sour cream
$1/2$ small cucumber, peeled and grated
$1/2$ tsp garlic salt
Pita bread

Season meat with 2 Tbsp garlic salt. Brown in skillet over me-dium-hot coals; drain. Meanwhile, wrap 6 pita pockets in alu-minum foil and place around the edge of the fire to warm.

To serve, remove pita bread from foil. Spread 1 tsp of Garlic-Cucumber Sauce (below) on the inside. Fill pocket with sea-soned lamb. Top with thinly sliced onion and more sauce. Serve with lettuce and tomatoes. Makes 6 servings.

Garlic Cucumber Sauce: In a small bowl, combine sour cream, cucumber, and $1/2$ tsp garlic salt. Cover and chill for at least one hour.

Lunchtime Pork in Pita

For Fat/Cholesterol-Modified Diets

$^1/_3$ cup cooked pork loin
1 Tbsp light mayonnaise
1 tsp spicy brown mustard
$^1/_4$ tsp lemon juice
Dash pepper
6 apple slices, cut $^1/_4$-inch thick
$^1/_4$ cup shredded lettuce
$^1/_2$ pkg pita bread

Trim and coarsely chop pork loin; set aside. Combine mayonnaise, mustard, lemon juice, and pepper in small bowl. Add pork, tossing lightly to coat. Stuff the pita pocket with apple slices, lettuce, and pork mixture.

The
Main Course

Fish and **Seafood**
Meats
Poultry

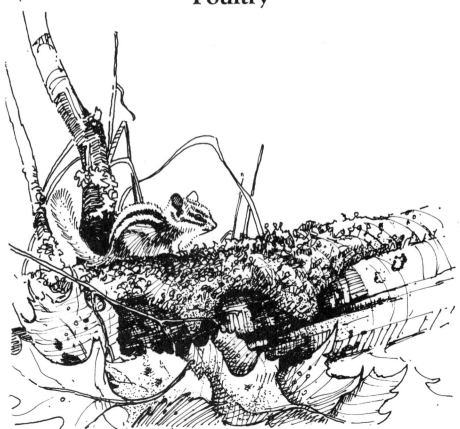

FISH AND SEAFOOD

Grilling Techniques
National Fisheries Institute

- A moderately hot fire is best for cooking seafood.

- Avoid strong fire starters and self-lighting briquets; their aroma can overwhelm the delicate fish flavor. Use an electric fire starter or kindling. Start the fire about 30 minutes before you intend to start cooking. Let it burn until white hot, then spread coals out in a single layer.

- Oil both the grill and fish to prevent sticking.

- For fragile fish, use a hinged fish basket. Or place fish on greased aluminum foil and poke a few holes in the foil, allowing the smoke to circulate.

- Cook fish steaks, fillets, kebabs, and shellfish directly over the heat source.

- Use indirect heat for large, whole fish. Bank hot coals on either side of the barbecue and place the fish in the middle of the grill.

- Baste fish frequently to retain moisture.

- When grilling seafood kabobs, all ingredients on the should cook for the same length of time. If necessary, cook shellfish and vegetables on separate skewers.

- Turn whole fish and steaks half way through cooking time. Fillets under one inch thickness need not be turned.

How to Tell When Fish and Seafood is Cooked

National Fisheries Institute

- Don't overcook seafood. Perfectly done seafood is moist and flavorful; overcooked, it becomes dry and tasteless.

- To estimate the cooking time, measure the fish at its thickest part, including stuffing, and allow 10 minutes per inch. A whole fish cooked by indirect heat will take 10-12 minutes per inch to reach an internal temperature of 140° F.

- Place fillets on the grill skin side down. If under one inch thick, the fish does not have to be turned. Otherwise turn half way through the cooking.

- Fish is done when it turns opaque and just starts to flake when tested with a fork but is still moist. Baste often during cooking.

- Shellfish such as shrimp, crab, lobster, and scallops turn milky white, or opaque, and firm when done. It takes about 3-4 minutes to cook through depending on size.

- Mollusks in the shell (oysters, clams and mussels) open when cooked.

Cleaning Fish

Now that you've caught a mess of fish, what do you do with them? First, keep your catch fresh. Keep the fish alive, or on ice, until you get back to camp. Then, clean them right away. DO NOT WAIT TILL MORNING. Otherwise, your catch will develop an unpleasant fishy taste.

There are several ways to clean fish. The method to use depends on the species of fish and the way you will cook it.

Skinning Catfish and Bullheads

Catfish and bullheads must be skinned. The following method does the job. Hold the head of the fish by nailing it to a board. Or hook your thumb and forefinger around the back of the front fins.

Secure fish; cut around dorsal fin

Cut through the skin along each side of the backbone, from just behind the head to just past the dorsal fin. Make another cut straight down behind the gill cover. Start where the first cut began and end behind the pectoral fin. Make this cut on both sides. These cuts should just penetrate the skin and not cut into the flesh.

Grasp the corner of the skin formed by the two cuts with a pair of pliers. Pull towards the tail. Skin should strip off one side. Repeat the procedure on the other side.

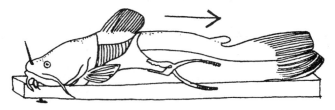

Peel skin toward tail

Once the fish has been skinned, it can be dressed. If desired, remove the head and fins. Now remove the meat by filleting, steaking, or prepare as is.

Cleaning Northern Pike

Northern Pike have many "Y" bones along the back of the fish. If not properly removed, a large portion of the meat is difficult to eat.

One way to clean pike is to first remove the fillets, following the methods for walleye. Then, remove the "Y" bones.

white "dots" — ends of "Y" bones

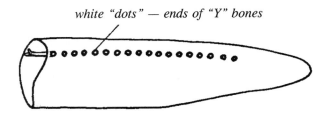

Look for a row of "white dots" which are the ends of the "Y" bones. You can feel these by running a finger over the fillet.

"Y" bone

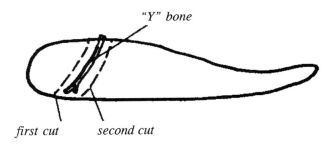

first cut   second cut

Using a sharp, short, flexible fillet knife, make a cut along the top of the "white dots." The "Y" bones curve slightly, so try to follow the curvature of the "Y" bones. Cut entirely through the fillet.

Make a second cut along the bottom side of the "Y" bones. Again, follow the curvature of the bones and cut through the entire fillet.

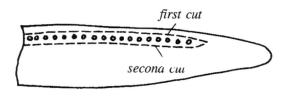

first cut

second cut

When making your cuts through the fillet, extend the cut toward the back of the fillet to the point where the "Y" bones end. This is near the vent. Beyond the vent there are no "Y" bones, which make these pieces good for the kids.

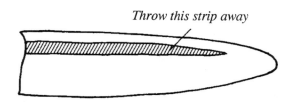

Throw this strip away

Cut off the strip of meat with the "Y" and discard. You should now have a boned fillet of Northern Pike. This process works best with fish in the 22-inch class or larger.

Filleting Walleyes

Place the fish on the cleaning surface. Hold the head firmly and **make the first cut just behind the pectoral fin**. The cut will be down to the backbone **but not through it**. Turn the knife towards the tail and cut along the backbone, through the rib cage to the tail of the fish.

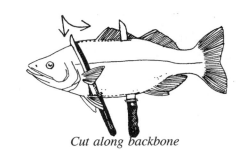

Cut along backbone

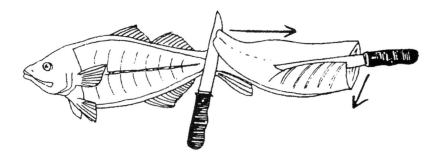

Place the fillet on a flat surface. Hold it down at the tail end. (You may have to use your fingernail.) Cut down to the skin, but not through it. Turn the knife towards the head. Apply some pressure to the tip of the knife by pressing down on the handle, forming a slight bow in the knife. Now cut toward the head, between the skin and flesh.

The last thing to do is remove the rib cage. Cut down into the flesh and turn the knife toward the ribs, cutting out the ribs. Wash the fillet and you are ready to prepare.

Crayfish

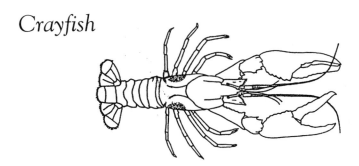

America's lakes and rivers offer several varieties of crayfish which are delicious to eat. Crayfish, or crawdads, are a favorite Southern delicacy, especially in Louisiana.

Purchase crayfish from local dealers or catch them yourself, using a baited minnow trap. Local game wardens and fish managers will tell you more about regulations and good trapping areas. Traps are made with a small-mesh wire screen, shaped into a cylinder about 2 feet long and 9-12 inches wide. A wire funnel with a 2-inch hole is placed at each end of the cylinder. Bait the trap with pieces of fish.

Keep the crayfish alive after the catch. They quickly decompose after death and the meat is mushy, discolored and inedible. Pack the crayfish in a tightly packed onion sack and store in a cool place. Never place live crayfish in small airtight containers, small containers full of water, or in direct sunlight, as this will kill them quickly.

Preparation

When preparing crayfish, first wash them, picking out any debris, bait, and dead crayfish. Some people like to add salt to the wash water to purge the crayfish. This only stresses them and is not recommended.

Cooking

Boiling is the most popular method of preparing crayfish. Use one gallon of water for every two pounds of crayfish. The pot needs to be fairly large due foaming water during boiling. You may have to boil several batches to meet your needs.

Season the water if you are planning to eat the crayfish immediately after boiling. Onions, lemon wedges, red pepper, garlic, salt, or commercial crab boiling spices are all good choices. Usually, one pound of salt will suffice for every five gallons of water. Alter this ratio to your individual taste.

To cook, pour the crayfish into boiling water, submerging all of them. When the water resumes boiling, boil for 5 minutes. Fully cooked crayfish will turn a bright red. Remove the crayfish from the heat, drain, cool, and peel. An alternative method is to remove the pot from the fire after the water comes to a boil. Set aside and let the crayfish absorb the flavors from the water for 10 to 15 minutes before draining.

How to Eat

Now you are ready to **peel and eat**. Two parts of the crayfish are edible - the tail and the larger claws. Because crayfish have a hard shell around the meat, remove it first. Here is how the professional peelers do it.

1. After cooking and cooling the crayfish, hold the tail just behind the head, between the thumb and index finger. Separate the tail from the head by slightly twisting, and firmly pulling, the tail from the head.
2. Next, hold the sides of the tail lengthwise between the thumb and forefinger and squeeze. Normally you will hear the shell crack.
3. Now grasp the first three segments of the shell from the side. Loosen and remove the shell by lifting and pulling it over the top of the tail. Discard the shell.
4. Finally, grasp the last shell segment and tail, and gently pull the tail meat out. You may have to twist it slightly. Remove the vein on the top of the meat.
5. Serve crayfish with your favorite sauce, add to a salad, or use like shrimp in other recipes.

Crayfish Creole

1½ cup cleaned cooked crayfish
2 Tbsp butter
1 small onion, finely minced
1 stalk celery, finely chopped
⅓ cup green pepper, chopped
1 tsp parsley
½ tsp salt
Dash of cayenne pepper
6-oz can tomato paste
1¾ cup water
1½ cup cleaned cooked crayfish
2½ cups hot cooked rice

Melt butter in a heavy skillet over medium coals. Add onion; cook until tender. Move the skillet away from direct heat. Stir in remaining ingredients, except crayfish and rice. Cook for 30 minutes, stirring occasionally. Add crayfish; heat through. To serve, pour over hot rice. Serves 4.

Crayfish Fondue

½ cup butter
1 large onion, finely chopped
⅓ cup green pepper, finely chopped
1½ to 2 lbs crayfish, cleaned
15-oz can cream of mushroom soup

Melt butter in a heavy skillet over medium coals. Add onion and green pepper; cook until onion is tender. Add crayfish; cook for an additional 12-15 minutes. Pour cream of mushroom soup over all. Stir constantly, until heated through. Keep warm. Dip pieces of bread into sauce for a hearty meal.

Variation: Seafood Fondue
Substitute 1 to 2 pounds of seafood (lobster meat, small cleaned shrimp, crab meat) for the crayfish. Substitute lobster bisque soup for the cream of mushroom soup.

Fried Crayfish

Flour
Salt and pepper
Crayfish, cleaned, washed and patted dry
Eggs, beaten (or liquid egg substitute)
Vegetable oil

Combine flour, salt, and pepper. Dip cleaned crayfish in beaten egg, then dredge in seasoned flour. Fry in hot oil until golden.

Fish

Basic Grilled Fish Steaks

Large fresh fish, cut into steaks
Extra virgin olive oil
Salt and pepper, to taste

Before starting grill, oil cooking grate with oil to prevent sticking. Brush fish steak with olive oil; season with salt and pepper to taste. Grill over hot coals for 4-6 minutes per $1/2$-inch thickness, turning once. Fish will be opaque and flaky when done; do not overcook. Serve hot with lemon juice or desired sauces.

Variation: Seasoned Grilled Fish
Brush steaks with olive oil, then season with fresh dill, rosemary, or basil before grilling.

BBQ Perch Fillets

1¹/₂ lb fresh perch fillets
Prepared barbecue sauce
Salad oil

Rinse fish with cold water and pat dry. Cut butterfly fillets in half. Generously grease a hinged wire grill. Place fish inside and baste with barbecue sauce. Cook 4 to 6 inches from hot coals for 6 to 7 minutes. Turn over and baste the other side of fish. Grill for another 5 minutes or until fish flakes easily. Serves 4. Serve with slices of buttered rye bread and fresh cole slaw.

Campfire Walleye Fillets

Walleye fillets
Butter
Sliced onion
Sliced fresh tomatoes
Salt and pepper

Butter a sheet of heavy duty foil. Place walleye fillets on top and cover with onions, tomatoes, and dots of butter. Season to taste. Loosely wrap fish in foil, sealing well. Place on the grill over medium-hot coals. When the top of the foil puffs, cook for 3 minutes more. Pierce foil to let steam escape, open, and serve.

Catfish

2 Tbsp bacon drippings
1¹/₂ lb fresh catfish fillets
¹/₂ cup cornmeal
Salt and pepper to taste

Heat bacon drippings in a heavy skillet over medium-hot coals. Season catfish with salt and pepper, then dredge in cornmeal. Fry in hot drippings for 4-5 minutes per side. Makes 4 servings.

Crispy Smelt

2 lbs pan-dressed smelt
  (approximately 15 per pound)
Salt and pepper
$1\frac{1}{2}$ cups flour
$\frac{1}{2}$ cup grated Parmesan cheese
15-oz can tomato sauce
Cocktail sauce and lemon wedges

Clean, wash, and dry fish. Sprinkle inside of smelt with salt and pepper. Combine flour and cheese. Dip fish in tomato sauce, then roll in flour mixture.

Heat oil in a heavy skillet over medium-hot coals. Place fish in a single layer in hot oil. Fry for 3-4 minutes or till golden brown. Fish will flake easily when tested with a fork. Drain on paper towels. Serve with cocktail sauce and lemon wedges. Serves 8.

Crowd-Sized Fish Boil

1 large wood bonfire
150 small red potatoes
100 small-medium white onions
100 lbs trout, salmon or northern
7 lbs pickling and canning salt
5 lbs butter
1 can whole pickling spice, tied in
Cheesecloth or an old, clean nylon

Set a large open kettle over a hot bonfire. Bring 30-40 gallons of water to a rolling boil. Add salt, whole pickling spice, and potatoes. (Potatoes should be washed with skins on and pierced with a fork.)

When water returns to a rolling boil, time for 5 minutes. Add onions (peeled and left whole) and boil for another 10 minutes. Add fish (cut in $1^1/_2$-inch thick steaks, leaving the skin on.) When water returns to a boil, cook everything for 12 minutes. Drain water off immediately. Serve on individual plates with melted butter.

Family-Sized Trout Boil

Normally, the traditional trout boil is designed to serve a hungry crowd of 100 or more. This recipe will suit a camping family's needs.

10-12 cups water
$^1/_4$ cup salt
12 small whole red potatoes, skins on
12 small whole onions, peeled
2-3 lbs fresh, firm lake trout or salmon
Fresh dill weed
Butter

Bring water and salt to a boil in a large kettle or Dutch oven. Pierce potatoes several times with a fork. Add potatoes and onion to the water and cook for 15 minutes. Add fish.

When the water returns to a boil, cook everything for another 5-10 minutes, or until fish flakes easily. Carefully remove from heat and drain off water. Serve fish and vegetables with hot melted butter and fresh dill, accompanied by slices of dark rye bread.

Fish-on-a-Stick

1   2-4 lb walleye
24-inch picture hanging wire
1 forked green stick, approximately 24 inches long
Butter or **margarine (optional)**

Start the camp fire and build up a good bed of coals. Clean the
fish (head should remain intact), wash, and pat dry.

Skewer the fork of the stick through the mouth of the fish.
The "handle" of the stick goes through the body cavity. Wrap
the picture wire around the walleye and stick, starting at the
tail. (See illustration.)

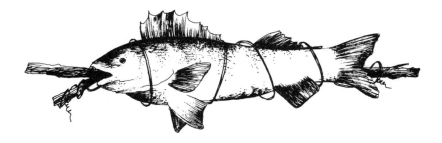

Suspend walleye, belly up, over the fire by setting the stick on
rocks surrounding the fire. Cook for about 20 minutes or until
meat flakes easily. Remove from fire. Peel back skin and remove
meat with a fork. If desired, dip fish in melted butter or margarine. This is a great recipe for shore lunch or when traveling
light—really delicious!

Fisherman's Delight

2 lb fresh pan-dressed small fish
2 Tbsp lemon juice
2 tsp salt
$1/4$ tsp pepper
1 lb bacon

Clean, wash and dry fish. Brush the inside of the fish with lemon juice and sprinkle with salt and pepper. Wrap each fish with a slice of bacon. Place in a well-oiled, hinged wire grill.

Suspend the fish about 5 inches from medium-hot coals. Cook for 10 minutes. Turn, and cook for 10 to 15 minutes longer, or until the bacon is crisp and fish flakes easily when tested with a fork. Serves 6.

Golden Fried Fish

3 lbs fish fillets, cut in serving size portions
2 eggs, beaten
2 cups flour
1 cup yellow cornmeal
1 tsp salt
1 tsp black pepper
Oil for frying

Rinse fish and pat dry. Combine flour, cornmeal, salt, and pepper in a flat pan. Dip fish in beaten egg, then coat with flour mixture. Heat oil in a heavy skillet. Fry fish fillets in hot oil, a few pieces at a time.

Fish is done when it flakes easily; flesh will be opaque. Drain on paper towels. Serve hot with a tartar sauce and lemon wedges. Makes 6-8 servings.

Grilled Barbecued Salmon

5 fresh thick salmon steaks
$\frac{1}{2}$ cup butter
2 Tbsp lemon juice
1 Tbsp Worcestershire sauce

Combine butter, Worcestershire sauce, and lemon juice in a small saucepan. Simmer for 4 minutes, stirring frequently. Brush each salmon steak with the butter mixture. Place the steaks in a well-oiled, hinged wire basket.

Grill steaks on an uncovered grill over medium-hot coals for 6 to 9 minutes, or until lightly browned. Again, baste each steak with the butter mixture and turn. Grill 6 to 9 minutes longer, or until fish flakes easily when tested with a fork. Baste often. Makes 5 servings.

Grilled Rainbow Trout

Fresh trout, one for each person
Salt and pepper

Clean and rinse the fish, and pat dry. Season to taste, or baste with selected sauce before, and during, grilling. Place trout on the grill, about 4-6 inches from hot coals. Allow about 1 to 2 minutes per ounce of fish. (Cooking time varies with the size of the trout and temperature of the grill.) Cook naturally folded, not open, (even if boned).

Trout will roll easily on its rounded back for turning. To remove from grill, slide spatula under trout from head to tail. Check inside the meat for doneness. Fully cooked trout will flake easily with a fork, with no pink remaining.
Note: Before starting grill, spray cooking rack with a non-stick cooking spray to help prevent sticking.

Trout Cooking Tips

- **Do Not Scale Trout.** A thin coat of natural jelly exists around the scales which allows the trout to be breaded without using any type of liquid.
- **Don't Overcook.** Trout should be moist and fork-tender. Overcooking dries out and toughens the fish. Trout is done when it flakes easily when probed with a fork.

To Bone A Cooked Trout...

1. Position the trout with the head facing left if you are right handed. Slip a table knife along the entire length of the backbone, steadying the fish with a fork in your left hand.

2. Gently lift away the top fillet, including bones and tail, and lay skin-side down on the plate.

3. Lift away bone structure and tail from the top fillet. Separate and remove head from the bottom fillet.

4. Sprinkle boned trout fillets with freshly squeezed lemon juice or cover with a special trout sauce.

Pan-Fried Perch

1 cup flour
1 tsp each of salt and pepper
2 eggs, beaten (or $\frac{1}{2}$ cup egg substitute)
2 cups finely crushed cracker crumbs
2 tsp fine herbs
Oil
Perch fillets

Combine flour, salt, and pepper. Put in a plastic bag and set aside. Combine cracker crumbs and fine herbs. Put in a separate plastic bag and set aside.

Heat oil in a heavy skillet. First, dredge each fish fillet in flour mixture, shaking off excess. Then dip fish in the beaten egg, and finally in cracker crumbs. Fry in hot oil until crisp and golden.

Salmon on a Skewer

1¹/₂ lb salmon steaks
1 medium cucumber, peeled
2 Tbsp green onion, chopped
2 Tbsp salad oil
3 lemons
2 tsp sugar
¹/₂ tsp ginger
1 Tbsp soy sauce
¹/₂ lb fresh mushrooms, sliced

Skin and bone salmon. Cut into 1-inch chunks. Cut cucumber in half lengthwise and remove the seeds.

In a medium bowl combine onion, salad oil, juice and grated peel of ¹/₂ lemon, sugar, ginger, and soy sauce. Mix thoroughly. Add salmon, mushrooms, and cucumber. Stir gently to coat. Chill, and marinate salmon one hour.

Remove salmon, mushrooms, and cucumbers from marinade. Cut remaining lemons into ¹/₂-inch slices; cut each slice in half crosswise. Thread salmon, lemons, mushrooms and cucumbers onto skewers, alternating fish with lemons and vegetables. Grill over medium-hot coals for 4 to 6 minutes. Turn and grill for an additional 4 minutes, or until fish flakes easily.

Scandinavian Shore Lunch

4 fresh trout
Salt and pepper
Dried dill weed
Flour
¹/₄ cup butter
³/₄ cup sour cream or plain yogurt
1 small cucumber, thinly sliced

Clean fish, but do not fillet. Season flour with salt, pepper, and dill weed to taste. Dredge fish in seasoned flour. Combine sour cream (or yogurt) and cucumber; set aside.

Heat butter in a heavy skillet over medium-hot coals. Fry trout until it is golden brown and fish flakes easily. This will be about 5 minutes per side, depending on the size of the fish.

Remove the fish to a warmed platter. Add sour cream-cucumber mixture to the skillet. Heat, stirring constantly until warmed through. Pour over fish. Serve immediately. Makes 4 servings.

Walleye Fillets Amandine

2 lb walleye fillet, cut into serving-size portions
Butter
1$\frac{1}{2}$ tsp seasoning salt
$\frac{1}{2}$ cup slivered almonds
2 Tbsp lemon juice
4 drops liquid hot pepper sauce

Place each portion on a sheet of heavy duty aluminum foil. Dot with butter. Sprinkle $\frac{1}{4}$ tsp seasoning salt over each fillet. Wrap fillets in foil, sealing edges well to keep in juices.

Place foil packets on a rack over medium-hot coals. Grill for 15 to 20 minutes, turning packets once during cooking.

Meanwhile, melt 2 Tbsp butter in a fry pan. Sauté almonds, stirring constantly, until golden brown. Remove from heat. Add lemon juice and hot pepper sauce, mixing well. Pour sauce over fish to serve. Serves 4-6.

Seafood
Basic Grilled Crab Legs

$1/2$ lb crab legs or claws per person
Butter

Arrange crab legs on the cooking grate over medium-hot coals. Grill, covered, for about 7 minutes, then remove.

To serve, crack open shells with a nut cracker. With a pointed knife, pick out the meat. Serve hot with melted butter or **Island Seafood Sauce** recipe (page 147).

Crab and Wild Rice

1 lb flaked crab meat
7 oz long grain and wild rice
2 cups sliced fresh mushrooms
$1/3$ cup salad oil
$1/2$ tsp salt
$1/2$ tsp white pepper
2 Tbsp extra dry vermouth

Remove any remaining shell or cartilage from crab meat and discard. Cook rice according to package directions in a large cast iron skillet. Add mushrooms 5 minutes before the rice is done. Add crab meat and remaining ingredients. Cook for two more minutes, stirring gently. Serve immediately. Makes 6 servings.

Basic Grilled Lobster

2 1¹/₂-2 lb fresh lobsters, cleaned and halved
   (claws cracked)
Lemon juice
Butter, melted

Before starting grill, oil cooking grate. Grill lobsters, cut side down, for 10 minutes. Turn, and baste liberally with lemon juice and butter. Continue grilling for an additional 10 minutes, or until meat is opaque. Do not overcook. Serve with additional lemon-butter sauce. Serves 2.

Basic Grilled Shrimp

12 large fresh shrimp, peeled and deveined
Lemon juice
Butter, melted

Combine lemon juice and melted butter. Before grilling, oil cooking grate to prevent sticking.

Grill shrimp directly over medium-hot coals for 3-4 minutes, basting with lemon-butter sauce. Shrimp will be pink on the outside and opaque inside when done. Serve with cocktail sauce. Serves 2-4.

MEATS

Beef

Braised Venison
or Beef Round Steak

3-4 lb venison steak
Flour
Salt and pepper
2 Tbsp butter
1 cup water
1 tsp instant beef bouillon
6 carrots, cut into chunks
2 stalks celery, cut up
Red wine

Preheat Dutch oven over medium-low coals. Season flour with salt and pepper to taste. Dredge meat in flour; pound in. Melt butter in dutch oven and brown meat slowly. Add water, instant beef bouillon, and vegetables. If desired, add a little red wine to taste. Cover tightly and cook over coals for 3 to $3\frac{1}{2}$ hours, adding water if necessary. Serves 4.

Cabbage Pigs in Sauerkraut

1 head cabbage
Lean ground beef or turkey
Uncooked instant rice
15-oz can tomato soup
Sauerkraut

Tear a head of cabbage into separate leaves, discarding the outer layer. Parboil leaves in water for a few minutes to make them pliable.

Combine equal amounts of ground beef and uncooked instant rice. Place 2 Tbsp of the mixture in a cabbage leaf. Wrap and tie with string. Place 1 quart sauerkraut in a heavy skillet. Pour tomato soup on top and cook over medium coals.

When the mixture starts to boil, drop the "cabbage pigs" on top of the sauerkraut. Cover and cook for 30-40 minutes, adding more water, if necessary. When done, remove pigs from skillet and discard string. Serve with sauerkraut.

Grilled Pizza

> **2 cups Bisquick®**
> **¹/₂ tsp salt**
> **²/₃ cup milk**
> **15-oz can tomato sauce**
> **Oregano**
> **8 oz meat (cooked sausage, ground beef, or pepperoni)**
> **8 oz shredded mozzarella cheese**

Combine Bisquick® and salt. Blend in milk and beat vigorously 15-20 strokes until stiff. Knead dough on a lightly floured surface. Divide the dough into four parts. Pat each part into an 8-inch circle.

Before grilling, oil the cooking grate to prevent sticking. Grill pizza crusts over medium-low coals for 5 minutes. When golden brown, turn. Cover toasted side with tomato sauce, meat, and oregano. Top with cheese. Grill 10-12 minutes longer, or until ingredients bubble and cheese melts. Makes 4 small pizzas.

Marinated Beef/Venison Tenderloin

1 whole tenderloin fillet (beef or venison)
$\frac{1}{2}$ cup soy sauce
$\frac{1}{2}$ cup red wine
1 Tbsp seasoning salt

Combine soy sauce, wine, and seasoning salt. Pour over tenderloin, piercing meat several times with a fork. Marinate in refrigerator or cooler overnight.

Prepare coals. Remove meat from the marinade sauce. Grill whole over hot coals 12-15 minutes per side for medium-rare. Slice to desired thickness and serve immediately. Serves 6-8.

Pocket Pizzas

The choice of toppings is as varied as your imagination. Make yours a gourmet pizza, vegetarian pizza, or use whatever is on hand.

2 pita pockets, halved
1 small jar pizza sauce
Shredded mozzarella cheese
Suggested Toppings (personal preference)
    Artichoke hearts, cooked, drained, and sliced
    Bacon bits, fried and drained on paper toweling
    Canadian bacon or pepperoni
    Green pepper, finely chopped
    Hot dogs, sliced
    Lean ground beef or Italian sausage, cooked & drained
    Mushrooms, sliced
    Onions, finely chopped
    Pineapple, crushed and drained
    Ripe olives, sliced
    Sun-dried tomatoes
    Sweet red or yellow pepper strips

Open pita pocket. Spread pizza sauce over the bottom half of the inside of each pocket. Top with $1/4$ cup cheese and desired toppings. Wrap each pocket pizza individually in heavy duty foil and seal tightly.

Place in medium coals and cook for 5-8 minutes. Remove from heat with tongs and carefully unwrap. They will be very hot! Serve with garlic bread and a nice salad to make a great Italian meal. Makes 4 pocket pizzas.

Pot in a Pit

1 beef or pork roast
Potatoes and carrots
2 medium onions
1 packet onion soup mix
1 cup water
Choice of seasonings

Place roast in a large Dutch oven. Clean and quarter potatoes, carrots, and onion; arrange over the meat. Combine onion soup mix and seasonings with one cup of water. Pour over vegetables.

Dig a hole at least $2^{1}/_{2}$ feet deep. Line with rocks (if available) and hot coals. Set the Dutch oven in the hole and cover with more hot coals. Cover the pit with at least 8 inches of earth, leaving the wire handle of the Dutch oven upright. Be sure handle is completely covered with earth. Leave pot in the pit at least 6 hours. Excavate your meal carefully and enjoy.

Warning: Be sure to lift the Dutch oven by the correct handles or you will lift the lid and not the pot. Serves 4-6.

Variation: Instead of digging a pit, place the Dutch oven in the middle of the hot coals from a campfire. Then cover the oven carefully with hot coals.

Skillet Meal

1 lb ground beef
1 Tbsp vegetable oil
1 pkg onion soup mix
6-oz pkg noodles
2 cups water
1 can mixed peas and carrots

Brown meat in oil in a heavy skillet. Add onion soup mix, noodles, and 2 cups of water. Cover and simmer 20-25 minutes. Spread peas and carrots over mixture and cook an additional 5-7 minutes. Serves 4-6.

Stuffed Peppers

6 green peppers, tops and seeds removed
2 cups cooked rice
2 Tbsp butter
1 lb ground beef
1 small onion, finely chopped
$^{1}/_{4}$ to $^{1}/_{2}$ cup chili sauce
Salt to taste

Boil the pepper shells for five minutes in lightly salted water; drain. Combine remaining ingredients and stuff peppers. Wrap in a double layer of heavy duty aluminum foil and bake in medium-hot coals for 20-30 minutes, turning occasionally.

Supper Wrap-Up

For each person have:

    1 hamburger patty (or hot dog)
    2 onion slices (top & bottom of burger)
    Carrot slices
    Potato wedges
    Strips of green pepper
    Salt and pepper to taste
    $1/4$ tsp water

Put all onto a sheet of heavy duty aluminum foil. Wrap and seal tightly. Place at the edge of the fire. Cook approximately 1 hour, or until vegetables are tender, turning occasionally.

Pork

Apple-Glazed Pork Kebobs

    1 lb boneless pork loin, cut into cubes
    2 Tbsp lemon juice
    Salt, to taste

Sprinkle lemon juice and salt evenly over pork cubes. Thread pork onto skewers and spoon apple glaze over all. Grill over hot coals for 10 to 12 minutes, turning and basting frequently.

Apple Glaze: In small saucepan, combine 1 cup apple jelly, 2 Tbsp lemon juice, 1 tsp cinnamon, and 2 Tbsp butter. Simmer until well blended. Makes $1^1/4$ cups sauce.

BBQ Special Ribs

1 Tbsp celery seed
1 Tbsp chili powder
$^1/_4$ cup brown sugar
1 Tbsp salt
1 tsp paprika
$2^1/_2$ lb loin back ribs
8-oz can tomato sauce
$^1/_4$ cup vinegar

Combine first five ingredients. Rub $^1/_3$ of the mixture on ribs. To remaining mixture, add tomato sauce and vinegar. Heat and use to baste ribs. Cook meat over hot coals until tender, basting occasionally with the sauce. Makes 4 servings.

Barbecue Ribs

1 Tbsp dry onion
2 Tbsp molasses
2 Tbsp vinegar
$1^1/_2$ tsp salt
8 oz tomato sauce
2-4 lbs short ribs

Combine first five ingredients. Pour over ribs in a dutch oven and cook in hot coals for 2-4 hours. Add water if necessary. This sauce is also very good with chicken. Serves 4-6.

Grilled Ham Steak

Grill a 1 lb ham steak over medium coals for about 2 minutes on each side, or until lightly browned. If a glaze is desired, brush pineapple preserves or maple syrup on ham during grilling.

Hobo Dinner

8-10 ears corn on the cob, cleaned
12 small red potatoes
1$^{1}/_{2}$-2 lbs Italian or Polish sausage
1 cup butter or margarine, melted
1 pint half & half®
Salt and pepper to taste

Arrange cleaned corn around the perimeter of a 1-gallon, metal potato chip can with the ears standing on end. Fill the middle of the can with potatoes. Coil sausage over potatoes and corn. Add remaining ingredients. Cover can and punch a hole in the top. Nestle the can over medium-hot coals until steam emits from the hole. Steam for 20 minutes. Remove meat and vegetables with tongs. Serves 4-6.

Hints: Reserve cooking liquid to pour over the corn. This meal can be prepared and frozen until time for your barbecue.

Macaroni Hot Dish

$^{1}/_{2}$ cup vegetable oil
8-oz pkg elbow macaroni, uncooked
1 small onion, chopped
$^{1}/_{2}$ green pepper, chopped
1 clove garlic, minced
1 cup cubed, fully cooked ham
$1^{1}/_{2}$ tsp Worcestershire sauce
3 cups tomato juice
Salt and pepper

Heat oil in heavy skillet over medium-hot coals. Add macaroni, onion, green pepper, and garlic. Sauté in oil until macaroni turns yellow. Add ham, Worcestershire sauce, and tomato juice. Season with salt and pepper to taste. Bring to a boil, stirring occasionally. Move skillet away from direct heat. Cover and simmer for 25 minutes. Serves 4.

Variation: Vegetarian Hot Dish
Prepare as above, but omit ham.

Marinated Pork Tenderloin

2 pork tenderloins, cut into chunks
2 cans frozen orange juice concentrate
1 cup brown sugar

Cut tenderloins into chunks. Combine orange juice and brown sugar in a 9 x 13-inch pan. Chill, and marinate pork in sweetened juice for 4-5 hours, turning occasionally. Place meat on the grill and baste with marinade while cooking, about 20-30 minutes.

Pork Spareribs

5 lbs pork spareribs or pork loin back ribs
1$\frac{1}{2}$ cups hickory smoke-flavored BBQ sauce

Cut ribs into 4 to 5-rib portions. In a covered grill arrange medium-hot coals around drip pan. Place ribs on the grill rack over drip pan, cover, and grill 30-45 minutes. Turn meat, brush with barbecue sauce, and continue grilling until ribs are thoroughly cooked, basting once or twice. Heat remaining sauce to serve with ribs, if desired. Makes 4 servings.

Lamb
Cranberry Lamb Steaks

16 oz jellied cranberry sauce
$\frac{1}{2}$ cup dry white wine
$\frac{1}{2}$ tsp ground cinnamon
$\frac{1}{8}$ tsp ground cloves
4 lamb sirloin steaks, 1 inch thick

Combine first four ingredients in a 1$\frac{1}{2}$ quart saucepan. Cook over medium coals for 8 to 10 minutes. Grill steaks over medium coals 10-12 minutes, turning several times. Brush with sauce during the final 5 minutes. Serve remaining cranberry sauce with steaks. Makes 4 servings.

Venison
Braised Venison Steak
(See page 106 for recipe)

Foil Venison

1-2 venison steaks
2 Tbsp butter
Carrots
Potatoes
Onions
1 Tbsp Worcestershire sauce

Arrange venison steaks on double thickness of aluminum foil. Place a pat of butter both on top and underneath the steaks. Add thinly sliced onions, sliced potato, and carrot strips. Top with 1 Tbsp Worcestershire sauce. Close the foil around the food; seal tightly. Bake in medium coals for 30-45 minutes, or until vegetables are tender.

Marinated Venison Tenderloin
(See page 108 for recipe)

POULTRY

Common Types of Poultry

Capon

Capons are delicately flavored young roosters weighing 6 to 7 pounds. They have a proportionally large amount of white meat. Roasting in a Dutch oven brings out the best flavor.

Chicken

Chickens are by far the most common type of poultry in North America. There are many types.

Broiling/Frying Chickens are small, tender chickens weighing approximately $1^1/_2$ to 4 pounds. Left whole, they are ideal for barbecuing or for the rotisserie. Bake, broil, grill, or sauté the cut-up pieces.

Roasting Chickens are a little larger chicken, usually weighing $2^1/_2$ to 6 pounds. Barbecue whole on a spit over hot coals, or roast in a covered grill. This will bring out the best flavor of these tender chickens.

Stewing Chickens are older, tougher hens weighing 2 to 5 pounds. They also contain a higher percentage of fat. Use these chickens in soups, stews, and in Dutch oven cooking.

Cornish Hens

Cornish Game Hens, or **Rock-Cornish Hens**, are the smallest members of the chicken family. These plump, little birds are butchered when they are 6 weeks old and average between 16 oz and $1^1/_4$ pounds. Roast, barbecue, or rotisserie whole for the best flavor.

Ducks

Ducks may be domestically raised or wild. They average between $3^1/_2$ to 5 pounds and have a proportionally larger amount of dark meat. Domestic ducks or ducklings may be prepared the same way as a roasting chicken. If the duck is wild, cook in a stew or Dutch oven, with a sauce, or with added fat, such as bacon.

Game Birds

Grouse, **partridge**, and **ptarmigans** are game birds which are larger than quail but smaller than a pheasant. Stew, cook in a Dutch oven, or prepare with a sauce or added fat, such as bacon. Because they are game birds, they tend to dry out more quickly than domestic poultry.

Turkey

Turkeys are the largest of the common types of poultry. They range from 4 to 9 pounds for a small or young turkey and 10 to 24 pounds for a large or mature tom. Unless you are cooking for a crowd, the small turkeys are the most practical for outdoor cooking. Stuff and roast whole, or cook in a covered grill. Leftover turkey may be used in an endless variety of recipes or sandwiches.

Take Care Against Salmonella

Salmonella is a potentially harmful bacteria that often grows in many foods, especially eggs, seafood, pork, and poultry. It resists cold and can survive for long periods. Wash poultry before preparing, then be sure to wash your hands and all cutting boards and utensils in hot soapy water before coming into contact with other foods. The bacteria can be killed easily by cooking the food completely. Poultry is completely cooked when a fork can be inserted with ease and no pink remains in the meat.

Tips for Grilling Chicken
National Broiler Council

- The process should be leisurely, never hurried.

- Keep a close eye on chicken while it cooks to avoid burning.

- Light the fire at least 30 minutes before starting to cook so charcoal is ash-covered.

- Adjust the rack 6 to 8 inches from coals. Use about 1 pound of charcoal per chicken.

- Place chicken on grill skin side up.

- Place small parts near edge of grill.

- Apply sauce during last 30 minutes of cooking, turning chicken often and applying sauce liberally after each turning.

- Be sure chicken is well-done, not "rare" or "medium".

- Chicken is ready to serve if fork can be inserted with ease.

- Pat bird dry before cooking. More natural juices escape from chicken that is wet.

Cutting Up a Whole Chicken

National Broiler Council

A whole chicken normally produces 9 parts; two legs, thighs, wings, and breast halves and the back, plus giblets. Ample for 4 servings.

1. Place chicken, breast side up, on cutting board. Cut skin between thighs and body.

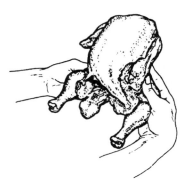

2. Grasping one leg in each hand, lift chicken and bend back legs until bones break at hip joints.

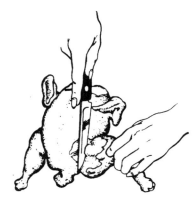

3. Remove leg-thigh from body by cutting (from tail toward shoulder) between the joints, close to bones in back of bird. Repeat other side.

4. To separate thighs and drumsticks, locate knee joint by bending thigh and leg together. With skin side down, cut through joints of each leg.

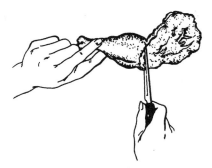

5. With chicken on back, remove wings by cutting inside of wing just over joint. Pull wing away from body and cut from top down, through joint.

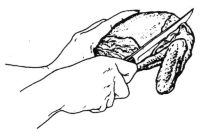

6. Separate breast and back by placing chicken on neck end or back. Cut (toward board) through joints along each side of rib cage.

7. Breast may be left whole, or to cut into halves, place skin side down on board and cut wishbone in two at "V" of bone.

Quartering a Chicken

National Broiler Council

Chicken quarters are ideal for backyard barbecuing. Convenient prepackaged chicken quarters are available at the meat market. However, it is easy to cut a whole bird into two wing-breast and two leg-thigh quarters.

1. Place chicken on back and, with sharp knife, cut in half along the breast bone.

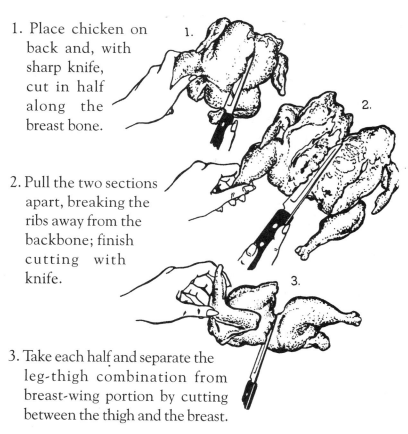

2. Pull the two sections apart, breaking the ribs away from the backbone; finish cutting with knife.

3. Take each half and separate the leg-thigh combination from breast-wing portion by cutting between the thigh and the breast.

Chicken

Chicken Fajitas

4 chicken breast halves, boned, and skinned
1 lime, juiced
$\frac{1}{4}$ cup pineapple juice
1 clove garlic, minced
Salt and pepper
Chili powder
Vegetable oil
Flour tortillas
Guacamole
Salsa

Place chicken breast halves in a dish. Combine lime, pineapple juice, and minced garlic. Pour over chicken; turn to coat all sides. Marinate about 30 minutes. Remove chicken from marinade, season with salt, pepper, and chili powder.

Brush lightly with oil. Grill over medium-hot coals until chicken is done. Remove from grill and slice into thin strips. Serve chicken piled in hot flour tortillas spread with guacamole and topped with salsa. Makes 4 servings.

Very Simple Version: Marinate chicken breasts in bottled fajita marinade or Caesar salad dressing. Remove from marinade, season, and grill.

Chicken Hot Dish

1¹⁄₂ cups raw rice
1 envelope dry onion soup mix
1 chicken, cut up
1 can condensed cream of mushroom soup
3 soup cans of water

Brown chicken; set aside. Combine rice and onion soup mix. Place in the bottom of a Dutch oven. Arrange browned chicken pieces on top. Combine mushroom soup and water. Pour over chicken. Cover the Dutch oven and bury in hot coals. Bake in a pit for 3 hours.

Chicken in the Garden

1 frying chicken, cut up
Medium potatoes
Tomatoes
Onions
Fresh mushrooms
Green peppers
Precooked packaged rice
Worcestershire sauce
Salt and pepper
Paprika
Butter

Prepare rice as directed on package. On a double thickness of aluminum foil, arrange 2 or 3 pieces of chicken, 1 pared potato, 1 sliced tomato, 1 peeled onion, 2 mushrooms, and 2 green pepper rings per person. Sprinkle with 2 Tbsp prepared rice, 1 tsp Worcestershire sauce, ³⁄₄ tsp salt, dash of pepper, and paprika. Dot with butter. Close foil and seal tightly. Cook over medium-hot coals for about 1¹⁄₄ hours, or until chicken and vegetables are tender, turning the package every 20-30 minutes.

Dutch Oven Chicken

1 stewing chicken, cut up
2 onions, sliced
2 stalks celery, cut up
5 carrots, cut up
2 bay leaves
1 tsp oregano
Salt and pepper to taste
Water

Arrange chicken and vegetables in a Dutch oven. Add seasonings and cover with water. Cover the pot and place on hot coals. Rake the coals over and around the sides of the Dutch oven, but make sure the handle is left exposed. Cook for about 3 hours. Serves 4-6.

Grilled Chicken

1 6 to 7-pound whole roasting chicken
Salt
$\frac{1}{4}$ tsp poultry seasoning
3 small onions, quartered
1 Tbsp rubbed sage
2 stalks celery, cut into 1-inch pieces
2 medium carrots, cut into $\frac{1}{2}$-inch pieces
3 Tbsp butter, melted
Desired barbecue sauce

Wash chicken thoroughly; pat dry. Rub cavity lightly with salt and poultry seasoning. Insert a few onion quarters in neck and fold neck skin over onion. Fold wings across back, with tips touching, to secure neck skin. Sprinkle 1 tsp sage in the body cavity and stuff with remaining onion quarters, the celery, and carrots. Tie the legs and tail together with string. Insert a meat thermometer into the thickest portion of the meat, not touching the bone. Brush skin with melted butter, and rub with remaining sage.

In a covered grill arrange medium-hot coals around a drip pan. Place chicken, breast side up, on a grill rack over the drip pan. Cover grill, and cook for $1\frac{1}{2}$ to 2 hours, or until the thermometer registers 185° F. Tent with heavy duty foil to prevent over browning, if necessary. Brush chicken with barbecue sauce during the last 15 minutes of grilling. Serve with additional heated barbecue sauce, if desired. Serves 6.

Lemon Chicken

1 3 to 4-lb frying chicken
Lemon Sauce, see below

Clean and cut chicken into serving pieces. Grill over hot coals for 30 minutes, basting with lemon sauce. Turn, baste the other side, and grill for an additional 25-30 minutes. Check for doneness by cutting into the thickest portion of meat. Chicken should be tender with no pink remaining.

Lemon Sauce
   $\frac{1}{8}$ **tsp minced garlic**
   $\frac{1}{2}$ **tsp salt**
   $\frac{1}{4}$ **cup salad oil**
   $\frac{1}{2}$ **cup lemon juice**
   2 Tbsp finely chopped onion
   $\frac{1}{2}$ **tsp each celery salt, pepper, and thyme**

Combine all ingredients in a covered, plastic shaker bottle. If possible, allow sauce to stand, refrigerated, overnight to let flavors blend. Shake before using. Makes $\frac{3}{4}$ cup.

Oriental Grilled Chicken

4 broiler-fryer chicken quarters
2 Tbsp prepared mustard
$1/4$ cup soy sauce
4 tsp honey
1 Tbsp lemon juice
$1/4$ tsp ground ginger

Combine mustard and soy sauce in a medium bowl. Gradually add honey, lemon juice, and ginger. Pour sauce over chicken, cover, and marinate in refrigerator or cooler for about 1 hour. Arrange chicken on prepared grill, skin side up, about 8 inches from heat. Grill, turning every 15 minutes for about 1 hour. Baste liberally with sauce during the last 15 minutes. Chicken is done when fork can be inserted with ease. Serves 4.

Zippy Grilled Chicken

4 broiler-fryer chicken quarters
1 pkg ($1^{1}/_{2}$ oz) taco seasoning
3 Tbsp light brown sugar
2 cups tomato juice
1 cup chicken broth
4 Tbsp vinegar

Combine taco seasoning and sugar in a small saucepan. Stir in tomato juice and chicken broth. Bring to boil over hot coals. Move pan away from direct heat and simmer sauce for about 8 minutes. Stir in vinegar and simmer 2 more minutes.

Pour sauce over chicken and let stand about 10 minutes. Arrange chicken pieces on the grill, skin side up, 8 inches from heat.

Turn and baste chicken with sauce every 10 minutes. Grill for about 1 hour or until done. Makes 4 servings.

Cornish Hens
Cornish Hens in the Coals

4 large Cornish hens
8 slices bacon
Salt and pepper

Select the largest hens you can find, and have them split in two. Salt and pepper to taste. Wrap each prepared hen in a slice of bacon. Cover with a double layer of heavy duty foil and bury in the coals. Cook for 15-18 minutes, then pierce with a fork to test for doneness. Adjust cooking time as needed. Serves 4.

Duck
Grilled Duckling with Cherries

1 5-6 lb duckling
2 cups apple cider or juice
Salt and pepper
Ground ginger
2 Tbsp flour
1 can (1 lb 4 oz) pitted bing cherries in syrup

Wash duck inside and out; pat dry. Sprinkle with salt, pepper, and ginger. Arrange hot coals on both sides of a covered grill, placing a drip pan in the middle. Grill duckling until tender (about 20 minutes per pound), basting frequently with apple cider.

Remove bird to a warmed platter, and strain drippings from pan. Blend together 2 Tbsp drippings with 2 Tbsp flour. Heat in a saucepan, stirring constantly. Gradually add the rest of the drippings, stirring until smooth. Add cherries and syrup; mix well. Spoon some of the cherry sauce over the duckling on the platter and serve the rest separately. Serve immediately. Serves 4-6.

Grouse

Stuffed Grouse

4 grouse, cleaned thoroughly
1 pkg instant stuffing mix, prepared
8 slices of bacon
Butter

Brown grouse in butter in a heavy pan over medium-hot coals. Place each bird on a double thickness of heavy duty foil. Stuff with prepared stuffing. Wrap each in 2 slices of bacon. Fold foil over bird, sealing seams well.

Place packets in hot coals for 60-70 minutes, turning occasionally. Grouse is done when a fork can be inserted with ease. Serves 4.

Turkey

Foil-Wrapped Turkey Dinner

1 precooked boneless breast of turkey, sliced
1 pkg instant stuffing mix, prepared
4 carrots, thinly sliced
Butter or margarine
White wine
Salt and pepper to taste

Prepare stuffing mix as directed. Place a pat of butter and $\frac{1}{2}$ cup of prepared stuffing on a double thickness of heavy duty foil. Top with one or two turkey slices. Top turkey slice with a little more stuffing. Dot with a small pat of butter. Next top with carrot slices and 1 Tbsp wine. Fold foil over packages, sealing well. Nestle packets in coals and bake for 30-45 minutes, turning frequently. To serve, remove packets from coals with tongs and carefully open foil. Season to taste. Entire meal may be eaten right from its foil package.

Turkey on the Grill

10-12 lb turkey
Garlic salt
Seasoning salt
Sage & onion dressing mix (prepared)
1 onion, minced
1 egg

Dressing: Cook turkey giblets in salted water with onion. Finely chop fully cooked giblets. Blend in one egg. Add to the dressing mix. Mixture should be fairly moist. If not, add a small amount of water.

Turkey: Season turkey inside and out with garlic and seasoning salt. Stuff bird and place on an aluminum foil pan with raised edges to hold juices.

Prepare covered kettle type grill. Make sure you have enough coals to cook the turkey. Once the coals are covered with ash, move half of them off to one side of the grill and half off to the other side (indirect method of grilling). Place the turkey in the pan on the middle of the grill and cover. After about an hour, juices should start accumulating in the pan. Baste bird frequently with juices, then turn bird carefully to brown all sides until done. It should take about 3 hours.

If desired, use a meat thermometer. Insert into the thickest part of the turkey before grilling. When the temperature reaches 180° F, the turkey is done. Remove the turkey from the grill and let it stand a few minutes. It will carve much easier.

Hint: If it looks like the ends of the turkey legs are browning too fast, wrap the ends in aluminum foil.

On the Side

Vegetables
Dips and Sauces

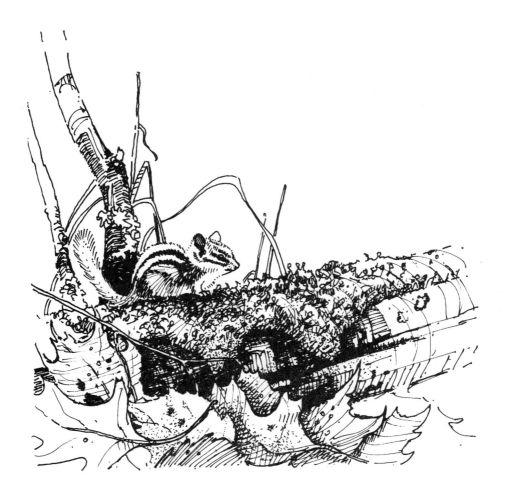

VEGETABLES

Beans

Calico Beans

$^1/_2$ lb lean ground beef
$^1/_2$ lb bacon, cut into small pieces
1 medium onion, finely chopped
$^1/_2$ cup catsup
1 Tbsp vinegar
$^3/_4$ cup light brown sugar
1 tsp prepared mustard
16-oz can pork & beans
16-oz can butter beans

Crisply fry bacon. Drain on paper toweling, reserving 2 Tbsp bacon drippings. Brown beef in bacon drippings; drain. Stir in onion, catsup, sugar, mustard, and vinegar. Blend in beans. Place in a dutch oven and cover. Bake in coals for 4 to 5 hours. Check occasionally, adding a small amount of water if necessary. Serves 6.

Corn

Chive Creamed Corn

3 oz cream cheese with chives
2 Tbsp milk
16-oz can whole kernel corn, drained

Combine cream cheese and milk in a small saucepan. Cook over low coals until cheese melts. Stir in corn; heat through. Makes 3-4 servings.

Grilled Corn on the Cob

Corn in Husk Method

Remove silk but do not remove husks. Soak ears in cold water for one to three hours. Remove from water and shake off excess water. Place on the grill over hot coals and cook for 30-40 minutes, turning several times during cooking.

Wrapped in Aluminum Foil

Husk corn; remove silk. Wash ears in cold water. Butter corn generously and salt, if desired. Wrap in aluminum foil. Place on the grill over hot coals and cook for 25-30 minutes, turning once halfway through cooking time.

Mushrooms
Basic Grilled Mushrooms

Fresh mushrooms
Extra virgin olive oil
Salt and pepper to taste

Wash and dry mushrooms and remove tough stems. Brush with olive oil and season with salt and pepper. Place on an oiled grill basket* and grill over hot coals for 4-5 minutes, turning occasionally.

*Grill baskets are available at many stores where outdoor cooking supplies are sold. They are constructed out of wire mesh or are perforated with many small holes, which allow the food to cook properly and juices to drain. Use grill baskets for small or delicate food items, such as vegetable pieces or small pieces of fish and seafood, that would otherwise fall through the cooking grate into the coals.

Portabella Mushrooms

Slice mushrooms. Marinate in one of the following for 1 hour in the refrigerator or cooler:

Olive oil, salt, and pepper
Lime juice, olive oil, garlic, parsley, and rosemary
Lemon juice, olive oil, cilantro
Italian salad dressing

Remove from marinade. Season with salt and pepper. Grill over hot coals for 4 minutes, or until soft, brushing with additional marinade.

Onions

Roasted Onions on the Grill

4 medium yellow onions, unpeeled
1 Tbsp olive oil
Salt & pepper to taste
8 tsp butter

Cut unpeeled onions in half through stem ends. Brush with olive oil. Arrange on an 18 x 18-inch piece of heavy duty foil. Season with salt and pepper. Top each with 1 tsp butter. Wrap loosely in foil, sealing edges well.

Grill onions on a covered grill directly over medium-hot coals for 20 minutes or until tender, turning foil package once. Unwrap foil package and serve. Serves 8.

Roasted Red Onions

2 large red onions, skins on
2 Tbsp salad oil
3 Tbsp cream cheese, softened
1$\frac{1}{2}$ tsp chopped chives

Brush unpeeled onion with 1 Tbsp salad oil. Arrange on a double thickness of heavy duty foil. Loosely wrap foil around onion, sealing well to keep in the juices. Repeat with the second onion. Combine the cream cheese and chives. Cover and chill.

Place foil packets on the grill over medium coals. Cook 45 minutes, or until onions are tender. Turn packets often.

To serve, remove onions from foil. Cut each in half and arrange on a plate. Top each grilled onion with a dollop of cream cheese mixture. Serves 4.

Stuffed Onions

6 medium to large onions
$\frac{1}{2}$ cup chopped ham
$\frac{1}{2}$ cup chopped green pepper
$\frac{1}{2}$ cup soft bread crumbs
$\frac{1}{3}$ cup milk
Salt and pepper

Remove a slice from the top of the onion; reserve. Hollow out the onions, leaving six little cups. Combine remaining ingredients and stuff onions. Place the top back on the onion. Wrap in a double thickness of foil and bake in hot coals for 30 minutes. Makes 6 servings.

Peas

Campfire Vegetables

Place one block of frozen peas (or other frozen vegetable) on a big square of heavy duty aluminum foil. Season with salt and pepper. Top with a pat or two of butter. Bring edges of foil up. Leaving a little expansion space for steam, seal tightly with a double fold. Place the package on the grill, or right in the hot coals, for 10 or 15 minutes, turning occasionally.

Minted Snow Peas

Its delicate taste is a perfect complement for fish or poultry.

> 2 cups snow peas
> 2 Tbsp butter
> 8-10 fresh mint leaves

Wash pods and pat dry. Arrange on a double thickness of alu-minum foil. Tear mint leaves in half and lay on top of snow peas. Top with butter. Fold foil up tightly to seal in the juices. Place packet on the grill over medium-low coals for 15 min-utes, turning packet halfway through cooking time. Serves 4.

Potatoes

Basic Grilled Potatoes

Scrub firm potatoes and dry. Pierce with a fork, and place on the grill over hot coals. Bake for about 60 minutes or until easily pierced with a fork. Turn halfway through baking time.

Cheesy Sliced Potatoes

5-6 medium potatoes, peeled and sliced
3 Tbsp butter
1 Tbsp mustard
$1/4$ lb shredded Velveeta® cheese
Salt and pepper to taste

Arrange $1/4$ of the potato slices on a double thickness of heavy duty foil. Dot with 1 Tbsp butter and $1/3$ of the Velveeta cheese. Repeat two more times and top with the last layer of potato slices. Wrap potatoes in foil, sealing all edges and seams. Grill foil packet over medium-hot coals, turning occasionally, until potatoes are fork tender, about 35-45 minutes. Serves 6.

Grill-Fried Potatoes

4 medium baking potatoes, scrubbed and dried
4 medium onions
butter

Make $1/8$-inch cuts into potatoes, being careful not to slice all the way through. Slip several thinly sliced onion sections between potato slices, place a pat or two of butter on top. Wrap in heavy duty aluminum foil, sealing edges well. Bake in coals for one hour, turning every 15 minutes. Serves 4.

Pizza Potato Topper

Baking potatoes
Bottled pizza sauce
Lean ground beef or Italian sausage
Shredded Mozzarella cheese
Sour cream

Scrub potatoes and wrap in foil, sealing edges well. Bake in hot coals until tender.

Brown meat in skillet; drain off fat. Stir in pizza sauce (1 cup pizza sauce to 1 cup meat.) Simmer over low coals.

Leaving foil intact, open potatoes; fluff insides with fork. Top with meaty-pizza sauce. Sprinkle on desired amount of Mozzarella cheese. Return to grill and bake until cheese is melted and bubbly. Serve each with 1 Tbsp of sour cream.

Potatoes Baked in the Coals

Potatoes
Sour cream
Butter

Scrub firm potatoes, rinse well, and pierce with a fork. Bury potatoes in hot coals for 45 to 60 minutes, or until easily pierced with a fork. Skins will be black. (If desired, wrap potatoes in aluminum foil before placing in coals. This will prevent some of the charring.) To serve, crack off charred skin and spread potato with butter or sour cream.

South of the Border Potato Topping

$^1/_2$ lb lean ground beef
$^1/_2$ cup taco sauce
1 cup shredded Cheddar cheese
$^1/_3$ cup crushed corn chips
2 baked potatoes, hot

Brown meat in heavy skillet over medium-hot coals; drain fat. Stir taco sauce into beef, simmer for 5 minutes. Open potatoes; fluff insides with fork. Spoon half of the meat mixture over each potato. Sprinkle with cheese and chips. Serve with extra taco sauce, if desired. Serves 2.

Sweet Potatoes/Yams
Grilled Sweet Potatoes

Sweet potatoes
Butter
Salt & pepper to taste

Parboil sweet potatoes until tender. Peel and cut in half lengthwise. Spread with butter. Grill in a hinged wire basket over hot coals, turning frequently, until hot and bubbly. Season with butter, salt and pepper.

Pecan-Glazed Sweet Potatoes

4 medium sweet potatoes or yams
4 Tbsp butter
$^1/_2$ cup brown sugar
$^1/_2$ cup pecan halves

Parboil sweet potatoes until skins come off easily. Slice potatoes into ½-inch thick slices. Place on a double thickness of aluminum foil. Arrange pecan halves on top. Sprinkle with brown sugar and dot with butter. Wrap tightly in foil and bake in hot coals for 20 minutes. Serves 4.

Sweet Potatoes N' Apples

4 large baking apples
4 medium sweet potatoes
4 pats of butter
2 Tbsp sugar
½ cup tiny marshmallows

Parboil sweet potatoes until tender. Peel and mash. Add butter and sugar, mixing well. Scoop out inside of apples, leaving a ¼-inch thick "cup." (Reserve discarded apple for making applesauce in the morning.) Restuff the apples with sweet potato mixture. Top with marshmallows and wrap in aluminum foil, sealing tightly. Bake in medium-hot coals for 15 minutes. Serves 4.

Squash

Foil-Baked Squash

1 summer or butternut squash
Butter
Salt and pepper
Chopped onion
Parsley

Clean and slice squash from stem to end. Scrape out seeds and stringy pulp. Fill squash with butter, salt, pepper, onion, and parsley, to taste. Wrap in foil and bake over glowing coals 40 minutes or in a reflector oven.

Grilled Acorn Squash

Cut squash in half lengthwise and scoop out seeds. Pierce inside several times with fork. In each half, place a pat of butter and a little brown sugar. Season with salt and pepper to taste. Place each half on a double thickness of aluminum foil and wrap tightly to seal in juices. Grill over hot coals 45-60 minutes, or until tender.

Variation: Maple-Grilled Squash
Omit brown sugar and add 1 Tbsp pure maple syrup. Grill as directed above.

Tomatoes
Grilled Tomatoes

> 2 large tomatoes
> 2 Tbsp extra virgin olive oil
> $1/_2$ tsp dried basil, crushed
> Salt and pepper

Arrange medium-hot coals on both sides of a covered grill. Slice each tomato in half crosswise. Remove excess juice and seeds. Dip tomato halves in olive oil and place in a foil pan. Grill covered, and using the indirect method, over hot coals for 10 to 14 minutes or until heated through. Sprinkle the cut surfaces with basil and a little salt and pepper. Serves 4.

Zucchini

Basic Grilled Zucchini

1 medium zucchini

Wash zucchini and pat dry. Cut in half crosswise, then each half lengthwise into quarters (makes 8 pieces). Chill, and marinate in one of the following mixtures for at least one hour:

Extra virgin olive oil, salt, and pepper
Olive oil, garlic salt, basil, oregano
Bottled Italian salad dressing
Bottled vegetable marinade

Remove from marinade. Grill cut side down over hot coals for 5 minutes, turn and grill for 5 more minutes, brushing occasionally with reserved marinade. If desired, sprinkle with grated Parmesan cheese during the last 5 minutes of grilling. Serves 2-4.

Reflector Oven Zucchini Parmigiana

2 lbs zucchini squash
1 envelope seasoned coating for chicken
$1/4$ lb shredded Mozzarella cheese
1 egg, well beaten
1 jar Italian cooking sauce
$1/4$ cup grated Parmesan cheese

Cut zucchini lengthwise into quarters. Then cut in half crosswise. Dip zucchini into beaten egg, then coat with seasoned coating mix. Place in an aluminum pan, cover with foil, and set in reflector oven. Bake near medium-hot flames for 20-30 minutes. Open foil carefully. Top zucchini with Mozzarella cheese. Pour Italian cooking sauce on top. Sprinkle Parmesan cheese over all. Cover once again and bake for 10 more minutes. Serves 6.

DIPS and SAUCES

Dips

Bloody Mary Dip

1$^{1}/_{2}$ cups sour cream
$^{1}/_{2}$ cup mayonnaise
3 Tbsp fresh green onions, chopped
1 envelope dry Bloody Mary mix
Fresh vegetables for dipping

In medium bowl combine first 4 ingredients; chill. Cut vegetables (celery, carrots, broccoli, cauliflower, or whatever) into serving size pieces. Serve with dip.

Chili Dip

2 cans chili without beans
1 can black olives, chopped
1 small onion, finely chopped
$^{1}/_{2}$ green pepper, finely chopped
2 jalapeno peppers, finely chopped
$^{1}/_{4}$ lb Velveeta® cheese, cubed
Tortilla chips

Combine first 6 ingredients in a large pan. Cook over low coals, stirring constantly, until cheese is melted and mixture is bubbly. Keep warm. Serve with tortilla chips. Makes a nice side dish to round out your meal.

Dairyland Dipper

16 oz cream cheese, softened
1 lb (4 cups) grated Cheddar cheese
$^2/_3$ cup sour cream
4 tsp horseradish
2 Tbsp grated onion
10 slices cooked, crumbled bacon
1 14-inch whole loaf or 3 4-inch round, whole loaves
   of rye or Pumpernickel bread

Combine first six ingredients and mix well. Cut a slice from the top of the bread and hollow out center, forming a bowl. Fill the bread "bowls" with the cheese dip mixture. Serve with crackers and fresh vegetable dippers. Makes 15-20 servings.

Marshmallow Berry Dip

$^1/_2$ pint marshmallow cream
1 Tbsp each lemon and orange juices
$^1/_2$ tsp grated orange or lemon peel
$^1/_4$ cup salad dressing

Beat together marshmallow cream and juices. Fold in lemon peel and salad dressing. Use as a topping for fresh berries.

Marshmallow-Cream Cheese Dressing

1 jar marshmallow cream
8 oz cream cheese, softened

Blend marshmallow cream and cream cheese in a small bowl. Chill. Serve with fresh fruit slices.

Nacho Dip

1 can nacho cheese soup
³/₄ cup shredded cheddar cheese
1 can chilies, finely chopped
1 cup milk
1 bag tortilla chips

Combine first four ingredients in a saucepan over low coals. Stir constantly until cheese is melted and dip is bubbly. Serve with tortilla chips.

Sauces

BBQ Sauce, Spicy

2 Tbsp flour
¹/₄ tsp ground cloves
1¹/₂ tsp salt
¹/₈ tsp pepper
2 Tbsp brown sugar
2 Tbsp Worcestershire sauce
¹/₃ cup chopped onion
1 Tbsp prepared mustard
¹/₂ cup vinegar
³/₄ cup water
1¹/₂ cups catsup

Combine first 5 ingredients. Blend in other ingredients. Simmer over low coals for 15 minutes. Brush onto meat while grilling.

Cucumber Sauce

$^1/_4$ **cup mayonnaise or sour cream**
$^1/_2$ **cup finely diced cucumbers**
$^1/_4$ **tsp salt**
$^1/_4$ **tsp celery seed**

Combine ingredients; mix well. Serve with fish or grilled meats. Makes $^2/_3$ cup.

Fresh Mint Sauce

1 bunch fresh mint leaves
$^1/_4$ **cup boiling water**
2 Tbsp sugar
Juice of 1 lemon
Salt and pepper to taste

Finely chop mint leaves. Add boiling water and sugar; let stand for 30 minutes. Stir in lemon juice, and salt and pepper to taste. Blend all ingredients well, then chill. Serve cold with lamb or wild game.

Honey Basting Sauce

Mix equal parts of honey and Heinz 57® Sauce. Use for basting meats and poultry while cooking.

Horseradish Butter

$^1/_2$ cup butter, softened
$^1/_8$ cup prepared horseradish

Drain and squeeze horseradish. Blend in butter. Serve chilled with grilled fish or beef.

Island Seafood Sauce

8 oz carton plain yogurt
$^1/_2$ cup mayonnaise
2 Tbsp catsup
1 Tbsp lemon juice
1 Tbsp minced onion
$^1/_2$ tsp celery seed

Combine all ingredients. Mix thoroughly and chill. Serve with crab claws or baked fish. Makes $1^1/_2$ cups sauce.

Lemon Butter Sauce

4 Tbsp butter
1 Tbsp lemon juice
1 Tbsp minced parsley
$^1/_2$ tsp salt

Melt butter over low coals. Stir in lemon juice, parsley, and salt. Mix well. Serve with baked fish.

Tartar Sauce

$^2/_3$ cup mayonnaise
3 Tbsp pickle relish
1 Tbsp grated onion

Blend all ingredients together. Chill. Serve with fried fish.

Tartar Sauce, Chunky

1 cup mayonnaise
$^1/_4$ cup sour cream
2 Tbsp each minced dill pickle and onion
1 Tbsp lemon juice
Dash of pepper

Combine all ingredients. Chill. Serve with baked or fried fish.
Makes $1^1/_3$ cups sauce.

Tomato Barbecue Sauce

1 8-oz can tomato sauce
1 Tbsp honey
1 clove garlic, chopped
1 Tbsp chili powder
1 tsp Worcestershire sauce

Blend all ingredients. Use as a marinade or basting sauce for meats.

Just for Fun

Kid's Stuff
Pie Irons

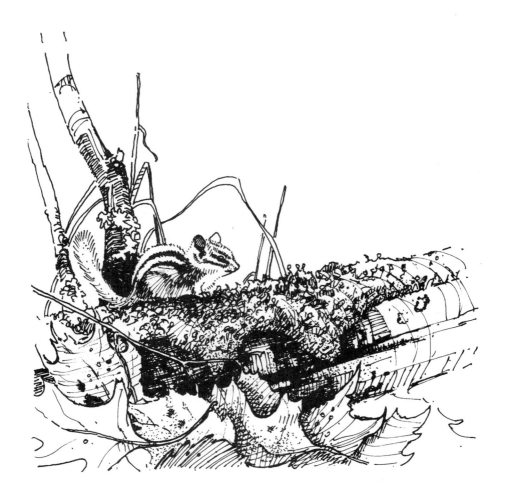

KIDS STUFF

Bugs on a Log

1-1½ cups bran flakes
2-3 Tbsp peanut butter
2-3 Tbsp honey
4-6 celery sticks
Raisins

Combine cereal, peanut butter, and honey. Stuff celery with mixture and arrange raisins on top.

Cherry Dump

1 can fruit cocktail
1 can cherry pie filling
1 bag miniature marshmallows

Mix ingredients. (Do not drain fruit cocktail). Chill and eat.

Child's Play

Fun and easy suggestions for nourishing snacks any kid would love

- Banana slices topped with chunky peanut butter
- Pear halves topped with softened cream cheese and nuts
- Pineapple slices with cottage cheese and seedless grape halves
- Bananas, sliced in half lengthwise, topped with whipped cream and fresh strawberries.

Finger Jello

4 envelopes Knox® unflavored gelatine
3 pkg (3 oz each) flavored gelatine
4 cups boiling water

Combine all ingredients and pour into an ungreased 9 x 13-inch pan; chill. It sets in one hour. Cut into shapes and serve.

Hate to Cook Chili

1½ lb lean ground beef
1 onion, chopped
4 cups water
2 cans Spaghettios®
1 can kidney beans
1 can tomato sauce
Chili powder

Brown beef and onion over medium coals. Stir in water, Spagettios, beans and tomato sauce. Season with chili powder to taste. Simmer till heated through.

Nutty Butter Sticks

1 Tbsp honey
½ cup creamy peanut butter
Chocolate chips or chopped peanuts
6 celery sticks, cut into 6" pieces

Blend honey and peanut butter. Wash celery sticks and pat dry. Fill celery sticks with peanut butter-honey mixture. Top with chopped peanuts or chocolate chips. Serves 6.

Peanut Butter Play Dough

This is a great recipe for the kids to make, play with, and eat—while you're relaxing around the campfire!

1 cup creamy peanut butter
1¼ cup instant powdered milk
7 Tbsp baby applesauce

Combine peanut butter and instant milk; mix thoroughly. Gradually add the baby applesauce, a little bit at a time, and mix thoroughly. If you want a stiffer dough, add a little more powdered milk. If you want a thinner dough, add a little more applesauce.

The children can now mold the dough into shapes and decorate their creations with chocolate chips, shredded coconut, or nuts. And they can eat their artwork.

Puppy Chow

12 oz semi sweet chocolate chips
1 cup creamy peanut butter
½ cup butter
17-oz box Crispix® cereal
2 cups powdered sugar

Combine first three ingredients in a medium pan over low coals. Stir until melted. Pour over cereal in a large bowl. Mix well until covered. Sprinkle with powdered sugar.

S'Mores

Graham crackers
Marshmallows
Plain chocolate candy bars
Nice campfire
Hungry kids

Sharpen the end of a green stick to a point. Spear a marshmallow, making sure the end of the stick pokes all the way through. Toast the marshmallow over the fire until it is a nice golden brown.

Place sections of candy bars on top of a graham cracker square. Top with the hot toasted marshmallow. Cover with another graham cracker square. The heat of the marshmallow will melt the chocolate. Eat and enjoy.

Peanut Butter S'Mores

Kids love this variation on an already favorite camping dessert.

Crunchy peanut butter
Milk chocolate candy bar
Graham crackers

Spread one cracker square with peanut butter. Top with a candy bar. Top with another cracker. Heat on a foil-covered grate over low coals (or in a reflector oven near hot flames) for 2-2$\frac{1}{2}$ minutes.

Very Simple Version
Omit peanut butter and milk chocolate. Top graham cracker with one regular-sized Reeses Peanut Butter Cup®. Top with another cracker. Heat as directed, or until chocolate melts.

Spoon Tacos

1 lb lean ground beef or ground turkey
1 onion, finely chopped
1 can chili beans
1 large bag of corn chips
6 oz shredded cheddar cheese
$1/2$ head of lettuce, shredded
2 tomatoes, chopped

Brown meat with onion. Add chili beans and warm slowly over low coals.

To serve, place corn chips on plate, top with chili mixture, cheese, lettuce, and tomatoes. Eat with a spoon.

Tomato Cannonball Sandwiches

2 firm, ripe tomatoes, hollowed-out
3 hard boiled eggs
Mayonnaise or salad dressing
1 Tbsp pickle relish
1 individual size pkg potato chips

Coarsely chop the eggs in a bowl. Stir in just enough mayonnaise or salad dressing to moisten (about 3-4 Tbsp). Stir in the pickle relish. Crush the potato chips in the bag. Fold into the egg salad mixture. Gently stuff the egg salad into the hollowed-out tomatoes. Wrap in plastic wrap or aluminum foil and chill until serving time. Serves 2.

Variation: Meaty Cannonballs
If desired, use one $4^1/2$ oz can of chicken meat or deviled ham instead of the eggs.

Tuna Schooners

1 small can tuna, drained
$^1/_4$ cup mayonnaise or salad dressing
$^1/_4$ cup chopped apple or celery
2 English muffins, split
8 triangular-shaped tortilla chips

Combine tuna, mayonnaise, and apple or celery. Toast muffins over low coals. Spread each muffin with $^1/_4$ of the tuna mixture. Insert the tortilla chips for "sails." Serves 4.

Watermelon Lady Bugs

1 slice watermelon
1 medium sized strawberry, stem removed
2 whole cloves
6 seedless grapes
Leaf of lettuce
Toothpicks

Cut slice of watermelon into an oval shape for the ladybug's body and put on a plate. Place the grapes, strawberries, cloves, and toothpicks into individual bowls. Insert a toothpick into the strawberry and then attach it to one end of the watermelon oval for the head. Two cloves will be the eyes.

Insert one end of another toothpick into a grape, taking care not to push it all the way through. Attach the other end of the toothpick into the side of the ladybug, making a leg. Repeat with the remaining 5 grapes. There should be 6 legs in all, three on each side. Arrange the ladybug on a leaf of lettuce for a cute and delicious salad.

Note: Supervise small children. Remove cloves, watermelon seeds, and toothpicks before eating.

PIE IRONS

A pie iron is a fun and easy-to-use utensil for cooking food around the campfire. It is constructed of heavy cast aluminum fashioned into a two-piece pan with a long handle. Depending on where you hail from, it may also be called a sandwich cooker or a pudgy pie maker.

Basic instructions are simple. Begin by preheating the iron over hot coals. Butter 2 slices of bread on one side. (White bread works best.) Spread 1-2 Tbsp desired filling between the slices, buttered side out. Position bread in the pie iron, close the iron, and trim crusts. Cook over the fire for about 4 minutes, turning occasionally to prevent burning.

A variety of fillings can provide you not only with a delicious desert but a warm breakfast, a quick lunch, and a hearty dinner. Here are a few suggestions to get you started. See how many more ideas you can come up with.

Bacon and Eggs

Bacon
Bread
Eggs

Cut each piece of bacon in half. Line the pie iron with bacon and top with bread. Crack an egg in between the pieces of bread. Close iron and cook over medium coals for 4 minutes, turning frequently.

Belgian Pie

A new way to create this classic, Door County, Wisconsin delicacy.

4-oz container crescent roll dough
2 Tbsp cream cheese, softened
2 Tbsp applesauce or apple pie filling

Unroll the crescent roll dough and divide in half. Each section will consist of two triangles. Roll out each half into a 5 x 8-inch rectangle. Cut in half to make two 5 x 4-inch pieces. Place one piece in each side of a buttered cooker. Place 1 Tbsp of cream cheese and 1 Tbsp of applesauce or apple pie filling on dough. Close the iron and cook over medium coals for 3-4 minutes, turning occasionally. Makes two pies.

Other Fillings For Belgian Pies
Cherry: For each pie use 1 Tbsp cherry pie filling and 1 Tbsp softened cream cheese.
Raisin: Combine 2 Tbsp raisins with 2 Tbsp cottage cheese. Use half of the mixture for each pie.
Peach: For each pie use 1 Tbsp strained baby food peaches and 1 Tbsp softened cream cheese.

Blue Plate Special

Rye bread
Butter
Baked beans

Butter one side of each piece of bread. Place bread in the pie iron, buttered side down. Spoon 2 Tbsp beans onto one side, close the iron, and trim the crusts. Cook for 4 minutes over medium coals, turning occasionally.

Chicken Pot Pie

Bread
Butter
Canned chicken stew

Butter one side of a piece of bread. Place bread in the pie iron, buttered side down. Spoon on 2 Tbsp chicken stew. Top with another slice of bread, buttered side up. Close the iron, trim crusts. Cook over medium coals for 4 minutes, turning occasionally.

Dessert Pies (Pudgy Pies)

Here's the classic recipe that started it all—fresh, warm pie to top off even the most basic meal.

Bread
Butter
Canned pie filling or applesauce
Cinnamon or nutmeg, opt.

Butter one side of each piece of bread. Place the bread in the pie iron, buttered side down. Spoon 2 Tbsp pie filling or applesauce onto the bread. Sprinkle with spices, if desired. Close iron, trim crusts. Cook for 4 minutes, turning occasionally.

French Toast

Give your family a warm start to frosty mornings at the campsite.

Bread
Butter
Milk
Eggs, beaten
Pure maple syrup

Butter pie iron. Beat together 2 eggs and a little milk. Quickly dip bread slices in egg/milk mixture and place in pie iron. Drizzle a little maple syrup in between slices. Close the iron, trim crusts. Cook over medium coals for 4 minutes, turning frequently.

Grilled Tuna-Cheese Sandwiches

$6^1/_2$-oz can of tuna, drained
Mayonnaise or salad dressing
1 Tbsp chopped onion
$^1/_2$ cup shredded cheddar cheese
6 slices bread, crusts removed
Butter

Combine tuna, onion, and cheese. Add enough mayonnaise to moisten. Butter one side only of each piece of bread. Place one slice of bread in the pie iron, buttered side down. Top with $^1/_3$ of the tuna-cheese mixture. Place another slice of bread on top, buttered side up. Close the pie iron and cook for 4 minutes, turning occasionally.

Ham and Swiss

2 slices bread
Butter
1 slice boiled ham
1 slice Swiss cheese

Butter one side only of each piece of bread. Place one slice of bread in pie iron, buttered side down. Top with ham and cheese and the other slice of bread, buttered side up. Close the iron, trim crusts, and cook for 4 minutes, turning occasionally. Dip in Dijon mustard for a little extra tang.

Hash and Eggs

Bread
Butter
Canned hash
Hard boiled egg

Butter one side only of a piece of bread. Place in pie iron, buttered side down. Top with 1-2 Tbsp hash. Top this with some chopped hard boiled egg. Place another slice of bread on top, buttered side up. Close the pie iron, trim crusts. Cook over medium coals for 4 minutes, turning occasionally. Makes a great, stick-to-the-ribs lunch.

Hash Browns

Butter
Grated raw potatoes
Grated onions
Salt and pepper

Combine potatoes and onions. Season with salt and pepper to taste. Butter pie iron and fill with potato mixture. Close the iron and cook over medium coals, turning frequently.

Pigs in a Blanket

8 slices of bread
Butter
Hot dogs, thinly sliced
American cheese

Butter one side only of each piece of bread. Place one slice of bread, buttered side down in pie iron. Fill with a few hot dog slices and strips of American cheese. Top with another slice of bread, buttered side down. Close the iron, trim crusts, and cook for 4 minutes, turning occasionally. To serve, dip in catsup and mustard. Serves 4.

Pudgie Pop-Tarts

8 slices of bread
Butter
Fruit preserves (strawberry, raspberry, pineapple—
   whatever you like)
Canned vanilla frosting

Butter one side only of each piece of bread. Place one slice of bread, buttered side down, in preheated pie iron. Top with 2 Tbsp fruit preserves and another slice of bread, buttered side up. Close the iron, trim crusts, and cook for 4 minutes, turning occasionally. Remove tarts from pie iron, and spread with 1 tsp vanilla frosting. Makes 4 pudgie pop-tarts.

Reubens

2 slices rye bread
Butter
1 tsp sauerkraut, drained
1 slice cooked corned beef
1 slice Swiss cheese

Butter one side only of each piece of bread. Place one slice of bread in pie iron, buttered side down. Top with corned beef, sauerkraut, Swiss cheese, and remaining slice of bread, buttered side up. Close the iron, trim crusts, and cook for 4 minutes, turning occasionally.

Shepherd's Pie

A quick, easy, and satisfying dinner when you've been out on the trail or water all day and don't have the desire to cook a big meal.

Bread
Butter
Canned beef stew

Butter one side only of each piece of bread. Place bread in the pie iron, buttered side down. Spoon 2 Tbsp beef stew in between bread slices. Close the iron, trim crusts. Cook over medium coals for 4 minutes, turning occasionally.

Shrimp Toast

Invite your camping neighbors over for a glass of wine and some appetizers before dinner. With a pie iron, these couldn't be easier.

8 slices bread
Butter
4$^{1}/_{4}$ oz can tiny shrimp, rinsed, and drained
2 green onions with tops, chopped
1 egg, beaten
2 tsp dry sherry
1 Tbsp cornstarch

Butter one side only of each piece of bread. Combine remaining ingredients. Place one slice of bread in pie iron, butter side down. Top with $^{1}/_{4}$ of the shrimp mixture and another slice of bread, buttered side up. Close pie iron, trim crusts. Cook for 4 minutes, turning occasionally. When done, cut into fourths, forming triangles. Repeat with remaining bread and shrimp mixture. Makes 16 appetizer servings.

Topping It Off

Desserts

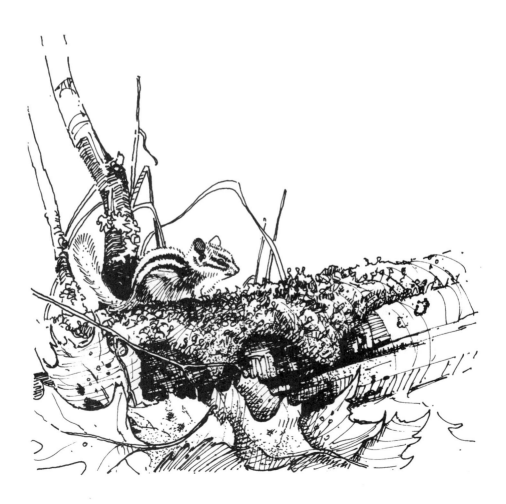

DESSERTS

Apple Cobbler

20-oz can apple pie filling
$\frac{1}{2}$ cup water
1 pkg refrigerated buttermilk biscuits
$\frac{1}{2}$ cup sugar
2 tsp cinnamon

Combine pie filling and water in a Dutch oven with a tight fitting cover. Cook over medium-hot coals until mixture boils. Boil one minute. Cut each biscuit into fourths and drop on top of bubbling apple mixture. Combine sugar and cinnamon and sprinkle on top of biscuits. Cover Dutch oven and cook over low coals for 20 minutes.

To serve, spoon warm cobbler into bowls. Top with whipped cream, if desired.

Baked Apples

4 apples, cored
Brown sugar
Miniature marshmallows

Peel each apple about $\frac{1}{3}$ of the way down. Place brown sugar and marshmallows in center. Arrange each apple on a square of aluminum foil. Bring foil up around sides and twist top. Cook over medium-hot coals for 20-30 minutes.

Variation: Reflector Oven Baked Apples
Place prepared apples in an aluminum pan. Cover with foil and slide into a preheated reflector oven placed near the campfire. Bake for 20 minutes, or until apples are tender. Move pan closer or further away from the fire to adjust heat if necessary.

Baked Apple Variations

Use any of the following combinations:

- $^1/_2$ Tbsp mincemeat mixed with $^1/_2$ tsp rum

- 1 Tbsp chopped walnuts and dried currants mixed with 1 Tbsp cream cheese

- 1 Tbsp chopped pecans and dried cranberries mixed with 1 Tbsp cream cheese

- 1 Tbsp raisins mixed with 1 Tbsp orange marmalade

- 1 Tbsp chopped bing cherries with 1 Tbsp chopped pecans

- 1 Tbsp chopped banana with 1 Tbsp crunchy peanut butter

Baked Caramel Apples

2 firm apples, such as McIntosh or Viking
Caramels

Core apple, taking care not to go all the way through. Stuff 3 caramels into the cavity. Wrap in foil, sealing well. Bake in hot coals or reflector oven for about 15-20 minutes.

Banana Boats

Bananas
Miniature marshmallows
Chocolate chips

Peel down one section of banana skin. Make a wedge-shaped cut down the length of the banana and remove that section. In the remaining hollow, sprinkle marshmallows and chocolate chips. Cover with banana skin. Wrap in aluminum foil and cook in medium-hot coals until chocolate chips and marshmallows are heated, about 5-10 minutes.

Caramel-Stuffed Pears

For each person:
   1-2 caramels
   1 firm pear

Slice a pear in half lengthwise and carefully remove seeds. Place caramels in the center, then place the two halves back together. Wrap in a double thickness of aluminum foil, sealing edges well. Bake in medium coals for 20 minutes or until pears are tender.

Chocoholic's Dream

$^1/_2$ **cup dark corn syrup**
$^1/_2$ **cup heavy cream**
6-oz pkg chocolate chips
Whole, fresh, ripe strawberries (or other fruit)

Heat corn syrup and cream in saucepan over medium coals. Bring to a boil. Remove from heat and add chocolate chips. Stir until chocolate melts and mixture is creamy smooth. Dip fruit in warm chocolate and enjoy.

Hint: Make this recipe while the kids are away or you won't get any!

Cinnamon-Spiced Apples

Large tart baking apples
Red hots cinnamon candies
Butter

Cut off a 24-inch length of aluminum foil and fold in half. Place cored apple in center of foil and fill hole with 1 Tbsp cinnamon candies. Dot with butter. Bring foil up loosely over apple and twist ends together to seal.

Cook over glowing coals about 30 minutes or till done. Serve with warm cream, if desired.

Coconut Ambrosia

8-oz can fruit cocktail, drained
8-oz can crushed pineapple, drained
1 cup miniature marshmallows
1 jar maraschino cherries, drained
1 cup sour cream
$^1/_2$ shredded coconut

Combine all ingredients together in a large bowl. Chill several hours before serving. Makes 8-10 servings.

Dutch Oven Cobbler

2 cans of fruit pie filling
2 boxes Jiffy® yellow cake mix, prepared

Preheat Dutch oven by placing ten or twelve pieces of charcoal under the oven with the lid on. Pour in two cans of fruit filling of your choice. Any combination of fillings can be used. For instance, raisins are good with apples. When filling starts to bubble, remove all but six or eight coals from the bottom.

Prepare cake batter as instructed on box. Pour batter on top of filling; cover. If desired, add chopped nuts. Sprinkle on top of fruit before adding batter.

Place ten or twelve hot coals on top of the lid and bake the cobbler until golden brown. The cobbler will cook from the top down. There will be just enough heat on the bottom to keep the filling hot without burning it. Aluminum foil can be used in the Dutch oven to keep it clean. This is also a good way to remove the cobbler from the oven for serving.

Fruit Cobbler

Line dutch oven with foil to the top edge of the kettle. Pour in one of the following:

3 cans (20 oz) prepared pie filling
3 cans (20 oz) sliced peaches with juice
3 jars (18 oz) applesauce

Prepare according to package directions:
1 regular size yellow, white, spice, or gingerbread cake mix

Pour prepared cake mix over fruit in the Dutch oven. Cover tightly. Nestle the oven in hot, glowing coals for 45-50 minutes. (Do not put coals on top of Dutch oven cover.)

Grasshopper Cookies

1 cup vanilla wafers, crushed
³/₄ cup pecans, chopped
1 cup powdered sugar
¹/₄ cup creme de menthe liqueur
2 Tbsp light corn syrup
6 oz pkg semi sweet chocolate chips

Combine the first five ingredients in a medium bowl. Blend well and let stand at room temperature for 30 minutes. Shape into 1-inch balls and place on waxed paper.

Melt chocolate over low coals. Remove from heat an cool to lukewarm. Dip one side of each cookie into chocolate and place on waxed paper until chocolate is set, then enjoy.

Honey Bars

1 cup of honey
12 oz butterscotch chips
12 oz chocolate chips
6 cups Rice Krispies® cereal
¹/₂ cup chopped peanuts

Heat 1 cup of honey in a medium saucepan over low coals. Add butterscotch chips and chocolate chips. Stir until melted. Pour over Rice Krispies® and nuts. Mix well. Pat into a buttered cake pan. When cool, cut into squares.

No-Bake Cookies

$\frac{1}{2}$ cup unsweetened cocoa
2 cup sugar
$\frac{1}{2}$ cup milk
$\frac{1}{2}$ cup salad oil
1 tsp vanilla
3 cup quick cooking rolled oats

In a pan over medium coals, combine the first 4 ingredients. Bring to a boil. Boil for 3 minutes, stirring constantly. Remove from heat. Quickly stir in remaining ingredients. Drop by teaspoonfuls onto waxed paper. When cool, store in an air tight container.

Pudgie Turtles

These turtles are gooey and rich enough to satisfy the most discriminating sweet tooth.

4 oz pkg crescent roll dough
4-6 caramels, cut into fourths
$\frac{1}{4}$ cup semi-sweet or milk chocolate pieces
4-6 pecan halves, coarsely chopped

Unroll the crescent roll dough and divide in half. Each section will consist of two triangles. Roll out each half into a 5 x 8 inch rectangle. Cut in half to make two 5 x 4 inch pieces.

Butter both sides of a pie iron. Arrange one piece of dough on each side. Top one of the sides with half each of the caramels, chocolate, and pecans. Close the iron and cook for 3-4 minutes, turning occasionally.

(More dessert recipes can be found in the Kid's Stuff and Pie Irons sections.)

Appendices

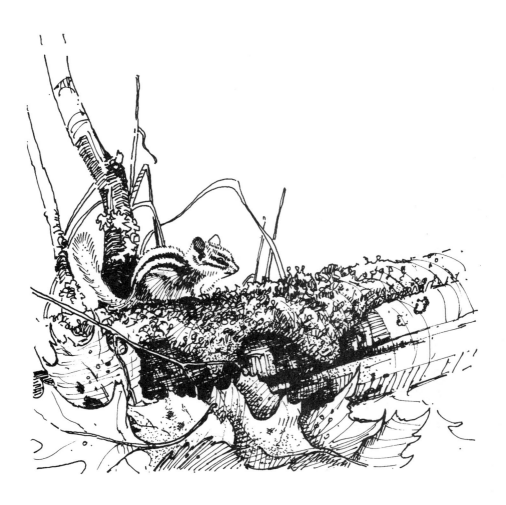

CAMP KITCHEN CHECKLISTS

Equipment, Supplies, and Utensils

- ☐ **Campground Cookery**
- ☐ bottle opener
- ☐ bowls
- ☐ can opener
- ☐ charcoal
- ☐ coffee pot
- ☐ cups
- ☐ dish cloth
- ☐ dish soap
- ☐ Dutch oven
- ☐ eating utensils
- ☐ fire grate
- ☐ first aid kit
- ☐ foil
- ☐ grill
- ☐ hatchet
- ☐ knife sharpener
- ☐ lighter fluid
- ☐ matches, waterproof
- ☐ measuring cups/spoons
- ☐ oven mitts
- ☐ paper toweling
- ☐ pie iron
- ☐ plastic bags
- ☐ plates
- ☐ pots and pans
- ☐ reflector oven
- ☐ sharp knives
- ☐ slotted spoon
- ☐ spatula
- ☐ stove and fuel
- ☐ strainer
- ☐ tablecloth
- ☐ tongs
- ☐ towels
- ☐ tripod
- ☐ water container
- ☐ weiner forks

Food Basics

- ❏ boxed dinners
- ❏ breads and buns
- ❏ butter
- ❏ canned meats
- ❏ canned soups
- ❏ catsup
- ❏ cereals
- ❏ cheese
- ❏ coffee
- ❏ crackers
- ❏ drink mixes
- ❏ eggs
- ❏ flour
- ❏ fresh meats
- ❏ fruits
- ❏ hot cocoa mix
- ❏ jams and jellies
- ❏ juices
- ❏ maple syrup
- ❏ marshmallows
- ❏ milk
- ❏ mustard
- ❏ onions
- ❏ pancake mix
- ❏ pasta
- ❏ peanut butter
- ❏ pickles
- ❏ popcorn
- ❏ potatoes
- ❏ powdered milk
- ❏ salad or vegetable oil
- ❏ salt and pepper
- ❏ seasonings
- ❏ sugar
- ❏ tea
- ❏ vegetables

TABLE OF MEASUREMENTS & SUBSTITUTIONS

Standard Measurements

tsp (teaspoon)

Tbsp (tablespoon)

oz (ounce)

qt (quart)

pinch	....	1/8 tsp
3 tsp	....	1 Tbsp
2 Tbsp	....	1/8 cup
4 Tbsp	....	1/4 cup
5 Tbsp + 1 tsp	....	1/3 cup
8 Tbsp	....	1/2 cup
10 Tbsp + 2 tsp	....	2/3 cup
12 Tbsp	....	3/4 cup
16 Tbsp	....	1 cup
2 Tbsp	....	1 liquid ounce

4 oz	....	1/2 cup
8 oz	....	1 cup
2 cups	....	1 pint
2 pints	....	1 quart
1 qt	....	4 cups
4 qts	....	1 gallon
8 qts	....	1 peck
4 pecks	....	1 bushel
16 oz (dry measure)	....	1 lb
1 liter	....	33.8 oz

Table of Substitutions & Equivalents

1 cup fine crumbs .... 22 vanilla wafers

....4 slices of bread

....26 saltine crackers

....14 graham crackers

1 cup whole milk .... $\frac{1}{2}$ cup evaporated milk + $\frac{1}{2}$ cup water

1 Tbsp instant minced onion .... 1 small fresh onion

1 Tbsp prepared mustard .... 1 tsp dry mustard

1 cup sugar .... $\frac{2}{3}$ to $\frac{3}{4}$ cup honey

....$1\frac{1}{2}$ cups maple syrup + $\frac{1}{4}$ tsp baking soda

1 whole egg .... 2 egg whites

....$\frac{1}{4}$ cup egg subtitute

1 cup sour cream .... 1 cup plain low-fat yogurt

1 oz baking chocolate ...... 3 Tbsp cocoa powder + 1 Tbsp oil

1 Tbsp fresh herbs .... 1 tsp dry herbs

1 Tbsp cornstarch (for thickening) .... 2 Tbsp flour

1 cup sour milk .... 1 cup sweet milk + 1 Tbsp lemon juice

1 lb apples .... 3 medium apples (3 cups sliced)

$\frac{1}{2}$ lb cheddar cheese .... 2 cups grated cheese

1 medium lemon .... 3 Tbsp juice + 1 Tbsp grated rind

1 medium orange .... $\frac{1}{3}$ cup juice + 2 Tbsp grated rind

1 lb potatoes .... 3 medium potatoes ($2\frac{1}{3}$ cup sliced)

1 lb tomatoes .... 3 medium tomatoes

INDEX